HARRISON TOWN

HARRISON TOWN

DISCOVERING GOD'S GRACE IN BEARS, PRAYERS, AND COUNTY FAIRS

BY MICHAEL W. NEWMAN

CPH™
SAINT LOUIS

Copyright © 1995 Concordia Publishing House
3558 S. Jefferson Avenue, St. Louis, MO 63118-3968
Manufactured in the United States of America

Library of Congress Cataloging-in-Publication Data

Newman, Michael W., 1961–
    Harrison town : discovering God's grace in bears, prayers,
and county fairs / Michael W. Newman.
        p.   cm.
    ISBN 0-570-048257
    1. City and town life—Michigan—Fiction. 2. Christian
fiction, American. 3. Humorous stories, American. I. Title.
PS3564.E91634H37 1995
813' .54—dc20   95-7715

1 2 3 4 5 6 7 8 9 10   04 03 02 01 00 99 98 97 96 95

To
Cindy, Hannah, and Abby: the most precious
family to be planted in
The people of Prince of Peace in Palatine,
who water me regularly
Charlie and Bill—great cultivators
My Savior, Jesus—Planter and Grower
extraordinaire!

CONTENTS

PREFACE

Everyone loves a good story. We learn from stories and relate to them. Stories keep our attention. That's probably why Jesus told parables. There was something important for the listeners to hear in those tales from real life. The stories in this book take place in a little town I'll call Harrison Town, Michigan. My family and I enjoy our vacation getaways there. You will read about all kinds of adventures and happenings. You will meet Ernest Thorpe, his family, his friends, and his pastor. You will laugh; perhaps you'll cry. These stories are not ordinary, however. They are stories of grace, God's grace at work in the lives of His people. They are stories that, perhaps, can direct you to Jesus' saving work in your life and show you in a practical way how you can live that new life. These stories bring God's Word into the reality you know: into the worry and wonder, the temptation and triumph, the sorrow and celebration. And just think, if the great work of the Lord can happen in Harrison Town, surely it is active and living in every area and every care of your life too! I give my sincere thanks to the people of Harrison Town, Michigan. And I pray that these will be stories of grace for you!

I

STORIES OF GRACE

· ·

GROWING UP

One thing you hear a lot about in Harrison Town, Michigan, is prayer. That's right, prayer. There's a lot of talk about it and a lot of it going on.

One of the pastors likes to hunt. He was hot on the trail of his favorite game when he came upon a bear, a *big* bear. As he reversed direction, he found the bear's partner. There he was between two big growling bears. It was a good opportunity to pray. The preacher's prayer wasn't eloquent, yet given the circumstances, he figured God would understand. He prayed, "Lord, I'm asking You to do all You can to make these bears, these bears that are Your own creatures, Christians in their hearts and actions." Suddenly it was quiet.

The preacher was encouraged until he looked to his right and to his left and saw the bears on their knees, saying, "Lord, bless this food we are about to receive."

Yes, there are many prayers said in Harrison Town. Probably a few more prayers than usual were said during the county fair—the 109th Annual Clare County Fair. No doubt the ladies at the Congregational church were praying for success for their fair dinners. They serve the best goulash and pie in town at a reasonable price. One of the husbands spelled the word *dining* wrong on the sign this year, so a few extra prayers might be necessary, they thought. And the chaplain for the Harrison Town Police Department had extra requests during fair time. The officers knew they would face their annual traffic jam—a tense time for everybody. First Street would be extra crowded this year, because country singer Randy Travis agreed to come into town.

The traffic wasn't the only problem, however. Fair week was the week when every boy who wanted to make mischief came out to show his stuff. A few years ago a boy named Ernest Thorpe was caught trying to dismantle the traffic-counter box chained to the No Parking sign on the road that led into the fairgrounds. As a last attempt at sabotage, he jumped up and down on the cable stretched across the street, so he could alter the traffic count. The city never did know if the count was accurate. That meant more stress and more prayers for Harrison's finest. And for Ernest it meant a police-car ride home to Mom and Dad, who were not amused by their son's fair-week creativity.

That event was significant for Ernest Thorpe. He couldn't see it coming—nobody could, but it would change Ernest's life forever. That bit of mischief got Ernest's mom and dad praying and thinking. How could they keep their son out of trouble in this small town? What could they give him to do? Mrs. Thorpe had an idea. Ernest would grow a pig! That's right. He would work all year raising a baby pig that was just about as stubborn as he was. Ernest would spend his days and nights grooming this pig for the week that was the high point of trouble in Ernest's life: fair week. He wouldn't have time for trouble. That settled it.

When baby-pig time came over at the Jacobson farm, Mr. and Mrs. Thorpe loaded Ernest in the truck and took him on a pig-picking expedition. Ernest was not enthused, so Mrs. Jacobson chose a pure, little pink pig to be Ernest's partner for a long while. The family stopped at the library to get some pig books and toted the whole load home to get started.

It was a busy time for Ernest. His mom thought she had created a future pig-farming enthusiast. But Ernest never really bought into the plan. Finally his halfheartedness got him into trouble. Two months before fair week Ernest *lost* his pig. He lost it! He left the pen open, and it was gone! It happened in a split second, he told his mom and dad. The pig just vanished! No one ever found out what happened to the pig, but Mr. and Mrs. Thorpe gave Ernest some time to think about the pig's fate during the next month of house confinement and cleaning.

On the last day of his grounding, with one-third of summer vacation gone, Ernest Thorpe was pretty frustrated. It wasn't the pig, or the lack thereof, or the chores that wore him down. It was his sister. When he finally let loose with a brotherly remark that implied he would have rather kept the pig and lost *her,* his sister rattled off a vicious list of reasons why none of Ernest's sports heroes would ever want to even shake his hand, and she closed her speech by telling him to go jump into Budd Lake.

That's the lake Cindy and I and the girls stay by. It's a small lake, good for all kinds of lake-type activities. It's also a lake that has some of the biggest muskies you'll ever find. For those of you who don't fish, a muskie is at the top of the food chain. It runs what goes on beneath the waves. He's big, and he's got teeth. And what a catch he is to fishing enthusiasts!

Well, Ernest was mad enough to take his sister's advice. It was time for a summer swim. Off he went to Budd Lake. He shimmied down the hill to his secret swimming spot, jumped off the rock that stuck out over a deep section of water, and cannonballed through the cool water right to the foot-high weeds on the bottom of the lake.

No one heard Ernest scream. Probably the only thing phased by Ernest Thorpe's scream was the muskie he found himself face-to-face with. Ernest opened his eyes after his cannonball jump, and there he was. He knew there were no submarines in that lake. The teeth were a dead giveaway. That muskie must have been at least five feet long! And that's about how high Ernest jumped out of the lake as he scrambled onto shore, regretting the moments he didn't enjoy with calm animals like pigs. He sprinted up the hill and started for home. That's when Ernest got an idea.

The sign he passed said this: COMING SOON: THE 109TH ANNUAL CLARE COUNTY FISHING DERBY. PLACE: BUDD LAKE. FIRST PRIZE: $100. Ernest stopped and thought. Who's gonna catch the biggest fish? The person who knows where the biggest fish lives! Ernest knew his mission. He would catch the muskie that lived in his secret swimming hole and win the fishing derby.

The next morning was Sunday. The Thorpe family got in their truck and headed over to St. Luke's Lutheran for the nine-thirty summer service. Ernest would be in confirmation class the next year, but it was still kind of tough for him to get everything out of church that his parents seemed to. Sermon time came. As soon as Ernest started getting real relaxed, he heard Pastor Graff quote these words of Jesus, "Ask and it will be given to you; seek and you will find; knock and the door will be opened to you." Then he heard about Abraham, who asked the Lord *six* times to spare the people of Sodom and Gomorrah. Abraham got the Lord down to 10 righteous people as the minimum number.

Pastor Graff preached on prayer. He made it clear that the Savior who gave His life on the cross and rose from the dead is the Savior who listens intently to our prayers. He talked not only of God's ability to do all things, but of God's love and faithfulness in saving our lives through Jesus in order to forgive us, to hear our every prayer, and to answer every prayer. No prayer is too big—Abraham showed that. And there is no prayer too small.

Pastor Graff said he didn't have to close the sermon with a stirring exhortation. Jesus didn't do that when He called every one of us to ask, seek, and knock; to trust Him with our lives; and to depend on the Holy Spirit's guidance in knowing His love. Ernest decided then and there that he was going to pray about that muskie. If God could consider saving terrible cities, and if Jesus Himself wants us to pray, the Lord could surely get that muskie to bite. That sermon really hit home, and Ernest formed another part of his plan.

He was unusually quiet on the drive home from church. He didn't even try to slide over and tighten his sister's seat belt. Ernest just looked out the window. He had a little less than four weeks to get ready for the fishing derby, and every moment counted. When he got home, he ate just a bit of lunch and went out into the garage. Ernest was going to make a giant "beno" fishing lure. It would be a perfect way to get that muskie's attention and hook him! With each wind of thread and hook attachment Ernest prayed, "Dear Lord, I want to catch that fish. I want to make my parents proud of me. I know You can do all kinds of things with people. You shouldn't have any problem with a fish. Lord, please let me catch that fish."

Around bedtime Mrs. Thorpe got Ernest out of the garage. She took his temperature and sent him to bed after giving him some Tylenol and rubbing Vicks on his chest. She wondered, Is he coming down with something?

Over the next week Ernest mustered up enough courage to ask his friend Andy Oreby whether or not he thought God could help somebody catch a muskie. Andy laughed and said, "Ernie, [Andy was the only one who called him *Ernie*] you can't pray for a fish! You can only pray for special big things, not the everyday stuff!" Ernest dropped the subject right away, but he didn't believe Andy. Andy thought the Ninja Turtles really lived in New York. Ernest decided to talk to his dad.

Mr. Thorpe was changing the oil in his truck. They had their differences, but Ernest knew he could talk to his dad. His dad prayed for lots of things when they had their suppertime devotions. He even prayed for Ernest. So Ernest asked, "Dad, can you pray for muskies?"

Mr. Thorpe stopped what he was doing and asked back, "What makes you ask that, Ernest?"

"Well, Dad," Ernest replied, "I can't really say right now, but I'm wondering if somebody could ever ask God to help him catch a muskie."

Mr. Thorpe didn't hesitate a bit. "They sure could, Ernest," he said. "In fact, it would probably be the best way to begin any fishing day."

Ernest's face lit up, "Great, Dad!"

Mr. Thorpe knew, though, that he had to get another word in. "But before muskies and such, Ernest, you've got to know who you're praying to. Remember, you trust God with your life. And you can trust His answer." Ernest left, praying harder than ever.

Finally the day of the 109th Annual Clare County Fishing Derby came. Ernest was registered. His equipment was ready, including his special lure. It looked like there would be some tough competition. Fishermen from all over the county gathered at Budd Lake. But Ernest knew his advantage. The biggest muskie he had ever seen lived in his secret swimming hole.

Ernest told his mom and dad to wait at the judges' booth, because he would have a great surprise for them. He started fishing and his homemade giant beno lure hit the water with authority. Ernest played the line just right. How could any fish resist the tasty morsel on the end of his line? Let the muskie see it a couple of times, get his attention, and Ernest Thorpe would be on the front page of the *Clare County Cleaver* as the fishing derby champion!

Mr. Thorpe ended up going to Harrison Town Lumber in the afternoon just to browse. Mrs. Thorpe waited for her son. Both were there around five-thirty when Ernest walked up to the closed judges' booth. He hadn't caught the muskie.

Mom and Dad took him to the new McDonald's. He got a number 3: quarter-pounder with cheese, large fries, and medium Coke. Ernest didn't feel like eating.

"Mom, Dad, I prayed," he said, "I prayed that I would catch that fish."

His mom and dad looked at him. They were proud as can be. They said, "Ernest, God answered you. That muskie was smart. But just think, Ernest, what would you have done without being able to pray to Jesus? His listening and love make a difference, don't they? The best thing you could have done was to keep praying and to keep trusting in the Lord's care."

Ernest finished his quarter-pounder with cheese. He was glad his parents were proud. He didn't even get in any trouble during fair week, and he was glad he had someone to talk to, the *best* one.

That night Mr. and Mrs. Thorpe heard a prayer coming through the walls of Ernest's bedroom. Mrs. Thorpe peeked in. She didn't see any fishing line or lures, just folded hands, a bowed head, and a boy having a heart-to-heart talk with his Savior. What a good summer it was for the Thorpe family. The 109th Annual Clare County Fair and Fishing Derby would be one to remember.

GOING OUT

Harrison Town is nestled around the shores of beautiful Budd Lake. One of the weeks my family and I go up to Harrison Town is fair week. I mentioned some of the excitement surrounding the fair. Of course, even when the fair isn't in town there is plenty to do. In June the Honda GoldWing motorcycle group comes into town. It's really something to see. They are a good bunch of people, and everyone enjoys the motorcycle parade around the lake on their last evening in town.

Throughout the year the senior citizens gather at the new McDonald's each morning for breakfast and conversation. And the kids love McDonald's. The restaurant features a train motif, with model railroad trains running around the top of each eating area.

Another hot spot is the Ben Franklin, where a good sale is always going on. Merchandise moves quickly, and there is always something new to see.

Right after the fair this year there was some excitement just across the street from the fairgrounds. A squad car with its lights flashing pulled behind a car parked on the street. The car's windshield was shattered. Turns out a golf ball had been hit right through it. There are three facts that make this event even more interesting. First, the car belonged to Mr. Ashcraft's son. Mr. Ashcraft owns one of the grocery stores in town and three other stores in surrounding towns. The car was a brand new Ford. Second, I was not the one golfing. It was Ernest Thorpe. And third, the monstrous drive that took out young Ashcraft's new windshield was hit at Harrison Town's miniature golf course, "Puttr Golf."

This was not a good day for Ernest. Puttr Golf was a hopping place. Many a date took place there, followed by an outing to the Dairy Queen. And this was supposed to be Ernest's first date. Well, it wasn't really a date. It was an outing with 10 other soon-to-be seventh graders. But Ernest liked Vicki Huber. He wouldn't admit it to anyone, but he wanted to impress her at this miniature golf outing. He saved his birthday money so he could afford the evening. He snitched a little of his dad's Old Spice aftershave. And when he stepped up to that sixth hole, he thought he saw Vicki looking his way. He didn't think the ball would get airborne like it did, and he certainly didn't expect to be talking to a police officer on his first date.

The damages cleaned him out. No more savings stashed in his baseball-card locker at home. The embarrassment didn't much help his self-image either. It would not be easy to face his friends. That meant he might not be able to go out with the group—and Vicki—for a long time!

Mr. and Mrs. Thorpe were not pleased with the result of this golf accident. They weren't bothered by the fact that it had happened. It was an accident. Accidents happen. What they had trouble with was Ernest's complaining. Why couldn't his family have more money like the Ashcrafts? Why did they have to live way down Spruce Street outside the city limits? The road wasn't paved, and it was so far from friends like Vicki Huber, who lived in town and much closer to the Ashcrafts. Why couldn't he get an allowance for all the chores he did around the house? Why couldn't he have good clothes and stuff like his friends had? It just wasn't fair. He wasn't satisfied with his place in life. That was no secret to the other members of the Thorpe family.

At supper one evening, as Ernest mumbled something about "chicken again," Mrs. Thorpe, like every good parent, decided to offer Ernest a solution to the problem. Ernest knew about his mom's solutions. Mrs. Thorpe said, "Ernest, I think it's time you got yourself a job."

Well, Ernest wasn't *that* serious about his complaints. But before he could object to the possibility of *working* during his free time, his dad chimed in, "What a great idea! I know just the place. Mrs. Paul needs some help picking apples and tending her land. I'll call her after supper."

Ernest swallowed his chicken and knew it was too late. Now he would never have any time to get to know Vicki Huber.

Mrs. Paul was an older German lady. She also lived on Spruce Street a little closer to town, but still outside the city limits. She was a widow. Mr. Paul died several years ago, and now she had to move. The house and the land were too much for her to take care of, and too expensive. This was not an easy time for Mrs. Paul. Mr. Thorpe made sure Ernest knew that, and he also made sure Ernest would be the most willing and cheerful worker Mrs. Paul ever met. Ernest was not happy with the arrangement, but if he tried to get out of it he would have to admit that his complaints were wrong. So he put on a happy face and hiked down to Mrs. Paul's the following Saturday.

It didn't take long for Ernest to learn the fine art of apple-picking or general cleanup at Mrs. Paul's place. And it really was a remarkable place! At one time it was a haven for all kinds of animals. There were birdhouses and bird feeders set up in special locations. The fruit trees and garden covered a large area. Mr. and Mrs. Paul were a hardworking couple. They loved to work together, and they loved the special place in the country they had built themselves. Mrs. Paul told Ernest all about it. She loved to talk and she loved to laugh. How then, Ernest wondered, could Mrs. Paul be without her husband, have to sell that special place, and still seem so happy? As the weeks went by Ernest never heard a complaint or saw her in a foul mood. He never heard her speak a negative word to her friends at church—she belonged to St. Luke too. Every Saturday she made Ernest a special lunch with homemade bread and fresh fruit, and all she talked about during lunch was how she was so blessed.

Ernest went home and decided to ask his parents about this. How could Mrs. Paul, an arthritic widow who has to move from her nice home, be happy? His mom and dad got one of those wise parent looks on their faces and replied, "Ernest, why don't you ask her?"

The next Saturday Ernest did. "Mrs. Paul," he said as he finished his delicious turkey sandwich, "I'm really glad to be helping you out. I know these are hard times for you. How do you stay so happy?"

Mrs. Paul really smiled then. "Ernest," she said, getting one of those wise parent looks on her face—why did all adults have to do that?—"it's my shoes."

Shoes? Ernest thought Mrs. Paul had said *shoes.* Mrs. Paul had a thick German accent. "Pardon me, Mrs. Paul," Ernest replied, "but I thought you said your *shoes.*"

Mrs. Paul laughed, "I did say my shoes, Ernest. You see, Mr. Paul and I had this little saying: 'We're not the only ones in our shoes.' Ernest, you can't leave our Lord out of the picture. He is with you. He knows your needs. And He has a special life for me. I'm not walking alone Ernest. Jesus is in my shoes too. My shoes!"

Ernest took the last bite of his turkey sandwich. He was thinking. Mrs. Paul went on. "Why do you think you learn what you do in Sunday school, Ernest? Jesus is real! He came to save you and forgive you and care for you as you get out into the world."

"But don't you miss Mr. Paul?" Ernest asked.

"Oh, Ernest," Mrs. Paul sighed, "with all my heart. Ernest, I have days when I feel terrible. But I know he's in heaven. That's why Jesus died on the cross. Mr. Paul wasn't the only one in his shoes. And I'm glad I'll see him again. I'm sure you have days when you feel terrible too, Ernest."

Ernest thought about Puttr Golf, and he agreed.

"I do not want to lose this house," Mrs. Paul continued, "but my life is more than all these things. Your life is too. Every time I feel cheated or sad or like an outsider, I look at my shoes, and I know that I'm not the only one in them. With the Lord, whether I have lots or just a little bit, I know I'll be all right, and I can be proud of the way God made me!"

Mrs. Paul took out a little German Bible. It was her husband's. She read two verses to Ernest, one from the Old Testament and one from the New. The first was from Ecclesiastes: "A man can do nothing better than to eat and drink and find satisfaction in his work. This too, I see, is from the hand of God, for without Him, who can eat or find enjoyment?" The second was from Luke: "A man's life does not consist in the abundance of his possessions."

"You're going out into the world, Ernest. You are a young man, and the world is very different from when I was your age. There will be many things you might want and feel like you're missing. But you will never really be happy, really content, unless you are thankful for your own shoes first. Do you know what I mean?"

Ernest thought he did. What an amazing lady Mrs. Paul was. Ernest finished his work that afternoon and went home. He was thinking about all his complaints. Even after paying for a new windshield, he had managed to save enough money to go on another outing with his friends that evening after supper. They were going to the Dairy Queen, and Vicki Huber would be there. Ernest got cleaned up. And before one of the moms came to pick him up, Ernest took an extra hard look at his shoes. He knew that the evening would be just fine.

SETTLING DOWN

Our little vacation spot is quite a town. Of course, I haven't covered all the adventure that takes place in Harrison Town. One period of excitement is imported by our family. It takes place on Sunday mornings at St. Luke Lutheran Church while we are in town. The odd and stirring event? Small children in worship. There aren't many little ones in the congregation. In fact, by my count there weren't *any* little ones in the congregation until we walked into that sanctuary that had no cry room available, no nursery, no doors to keep sound out, and no visible escape areas for the average parent wrestling with the average small child. It's one of those "best of times/worst of times" situations. It's great to be in church and worship with my family. It's great to be a dad teaching what this special time with the Lord is all about. But it was also a bit tense when most everyone kept looking back at us as if they had never before seen constant motion. It wasn't their fault. You tend to look where the action is. And this was new action for the folks at St. Luke.

That first Sunday was quite a worship service. I don't know what Pastor Graff said exactly. I did get the first three and the last three minutes of his sermon. And those were good. He is a faithful and effective preacher. By the time church had let out, however, I had really worked up an appetite and was ready for breakfast. I asked a few of the longtime Harrison Town residents where you could get a good Sunday breakfast. The Jackpine Restaurant was a favorite standby. There were some good breakfast deals down in Clare. And then there was the American Legion Hall just outside town. I remembered passing the hall on my morning runs and seeing the sign: SUNDAY BREAKFAST 9 A.M.—1 P.M. That sounded good. Why not give it a try?

We pulled into the American Legion Post 167 parking lot, ventured inside, sat down, and took a look at the menu. What a deal! The kids ate free. I ordered a number 4: three giant pancakes, a pile of scrambled eggs, and a bunch of bacon. Unfortunately, the kids thought we were still in church. And that doesn't mean they were sitting in worshipful positions. Now, a bunch of fellow Lutherans might get along fine with this twice-yearly adventure of little ones in their midst. They might even enjoy the novelty. I didn't want to press my luck, however, with a hall full of legionnaires trying to enjoy breakfast. So I finished my food in record time and headed toward the cashier. I'd have two hands free, and we'd be ready to bail out as soon as the girls were finished eating.

I paid, complimented the cashier on the delicious breakfast, and made some kind of comment that being a parent is quite an adventure. She replied, "Oh, I know. I've got 13 children." What? Thirteen children! I told her that she had my complete admiration. She went on,

"And I have 42 grandchildren." I could hardly speak. Thirteen children and 42 grandchildren!

"How did you do it?" I asked.

"Just like you are," she replied, "only a few more times."

I couldn't believe it. Here was a person who actually survived, a veteran, and she was still able to smile!

I asked her again, "How did you do it? What differences do you notice between then and now?"

"There are some differences," she commented. "Kids *want* a lot more nowadays. My grandchildren are always talking about something new that they want. Generally, though, things haven't changed much. Kids are still growing up and doing the same things they've always done. Kids don't change much. We're the ones who change."

"How do we change?" I asked.

"Well," she began in a knowing way, "there's a lot more you can worry about when you get older. You worry about the kids. You worry about the bills. You worry about work. You worry about being on time here and there. You worry about what other people think. You worry about the world. You worry about your health. There's a lot more you start worrying about."

I saw her point. "I guess so," I replied.

"How many times do you hear of *kids* getting ulcers?" she asked.

"Not many." She was right. I could see that in myself.

"So how did you do it?" I asked again. "I can't

imagine raising 13 children."

"I didn't do it," she answered. "The Lord did it. Sure, I was in there through it all—diapers, the terrible twos, school days, teenagers, growing up, leaving home. But I couldn't have done it without the Lord."

What a great witness to faith, I thought. So I asked, "How did He help you through all that?"

"He settled me down," she answered. "He settled me down. I wasn't perfect. I got worked up and worried and frantic like any other parent. But I had my Bible, and I had my faith. God let me know that He was doing His work. Jesus was close by me. 'Don't be afraid,' the Bible told me. That would settle me down when I got worked up and worried. I just had to trust Him. In the Lord's hands everything is easy."

Then she started talking about more than just being a parent. "Everybody needs some settling down! Abraham was 100 years old, and he still worried about his family. Moses worried about talking to Pharaoh. Joshua worried about leading God's people. David worried about being king. Jeremiah worried about being a prophet. Jonah worried about going to Nineveh. The disciples worried while Jesus lived, after He died, and after He was alive again! If you read the Bible you find a bunch of worrywarts—just like us. The Lord settled them down by what He did. He settles you and me down too—by what He's doing. That's what got me through."

I smiled from ear to ear. Wow! That was faith. Knowing that God was really doing His work. She was amazing.

She continued: "Of course, there are times when you have your doubts. Things happen that make you wonder. I've got a grandson I've wondered about on a few occasions. But when you're wondering, that's when you need the Lord to settle you down. Let me tell you, with 13 of my own and 42 grandkids, I still need to be settled down plenty of times."

I agreed. I needed that too. That morning was a perfect example. I finished paying for breakfast, told her that it was a real pleasure to meet her and to hear about her family and her faith. I went back to the table. We scooped up the kids. On the way out I told Cindy about the lady I had just met who really had her hands full: 13 children and 42 grandchildren! As we passed her again, I said thank you and glanced at her nametag. Emma Thorpe. Could it be? I wondered to myself. Ernest's grandma? Cindy and I hustled out to the car in the rain, got the girls inside, and headed toward the cottage. As we drove back I knew that I had heard another sermon at the American Legion Hall that morning. Faith. The Lord really does work. He's the one to settle me down too. I'm glad He is who He is, the dependable Savior who cares. I hope and pray we can remember that and stick to it like Emma Thorpe has.

Soon it was time for us to leave. It's good to get back home, and there is a lot of activity to go along with the trip back—the packing and the traffic. But it would be okay. No need to worry when the Lord is doing His work and settling you down—even as life picked up and we said farewell to Harrison Town, Michigan, nestled around the shores of beautiful Budd Lake. Until next year.

II

STORIES OF PASSION

STAYING STEADY

. . . .

"In the Heart of Michigan's Vacationland." That's
how the *Clare County Cleaver* describes Harrison Town.
During the winter months Harrison Town is a little town
that still bustles with activity. It's a regular winter won-
derland in north-central Michigan. Each winter the
"Hare Scrambler" Motocross competition is held in Harrison Town. The "Frostbite Open" volleyball tournament
provides thrills and chills for those willing to challenge
the arctic temperatures. The "Cabin Fever Variety Show"
provides a warmer climate for winter entertainment.
This year the big news in town was the purchase of a
new snowmobile path groomer. It even has a closed cab
so Gary Halas from the fire department won't get too
cold when he grooms those paths. And, of course, ice
fishing in Budd Lake is a big draw.

To young Ernest Thorpe, a seventh grader at the
new middle school in Harrison Town and the energetic
boy you've come to know well, all of those winterrific
activities could be described with one word: *boring!*
That's right, boring! Being in the heart of Michigan's
vacationland did nothing for him during the long, dark,

cold winters. Ernest liked summer. He liked to get out of the house and hike around in the woods. He liked to swim in Budd Lake. In the winter it was the same old routine. Every Sunday his Uncle John came over and cracked the same joke: he and his wife were in the iron and steel business. She'd *iron* and he'd *steal*. Ernest wanted a little excitement. And that's when opportunity came knocking.

It was Monday morning and Ernest sat at his desk. The students were in alphabetical order in the classroom. That meant Ernest sat next to Paul Tucker, the kind of kid all of us know at one time or another. His desk was a disaster area, and he loved it that way. He couldn't close his desk because papers from the beginning of the year stuck out the sides. His permission slip for the fall field trip was lost in there somewhere. Every time he needed a pencil he opened his desk, rummaged around, and pulled out half of one—broken from the karate demonstration he gave with all of his pencils. Paul tormented any girl that sat nearby. He mumbled while the teacher talked and made strange sounds when everyone was supposed to be quiet.

That Monday Paul Tucker knew that Ernest's attitude was at a low ebb. So he proposed an activity to bring a little spark to Ernest's dull life. It was science time. Why not put the worm they had just dissected into Nina Sorensen's desk? That would cause some excitement. Ernest consented. He carried the worm and Paul Tucker opened the desk.

But Mr. Black closed the desk! Mr. Black was the principal. He had a habit of looking in on classrooms throughout the day. Ernest Thorpe and Paul Tucker didn't plan on Mr. Black looking in on theirs just then. The result? Detention all week. Paul Tucker had some past offenses for which Ernest paid some of the price. Detention. Now winter was worse than ever!

Mr. and Mrs. Thorpe weren't happy about the situation. They found out about it before Ernest got home. They were in full support of the week of detention. After a long talk and a ruling of no TV the rest of the week, Ernest's attitude was completely soured. By the time Friday came he was ready for Paul Tucker's daring suggestion. On the way out of detention Paul Tucker whispered to Ernest, "Revenge, Ernest! Revenge!"

"What do you mean, Paul?" Ernest asked.

"We have to fight back, Ernest," Paul replied. "Did you know that Mr. Black has an ice-fishing shanty on Budd Lake? What if the entire floor of that shanty was augered out—holes everywhere!? Mr. Black might have a boring winter too!"

"When would we be able to do that?" Ernest asked.

Paul Tucker had the answer ready: "Monday is teachers' institute day. We could sneak over and do it then. Do you have an auger at your house?"

Ernest's dad's auger was in the corner of the garage. It could drill out the floor of Mr. Black's shanty any day. "Yeah," Ernest answered. "Yeah, I can get one."

"Okay," Paul Tucker strategized, "I'll meet you there at 10 in the morning on Monday. Revenge!" Paul Tucker smiled and walked toward home.

On Saturday Ernest didn't do much. It was his last day without TV. When his dad went on an errand, however, Ernest took his dad's ice-fishing auger and put it in his closet. He was ready for his Monday appointment with Paul Tucker.

Finally Sunday morning came. It was time for church. Sunday school was at nine and worship at ten-fifteen during the winter. At about five minutes past ten, Ernest, his sister, and his mom and dad sat in their pew ready for worship. Ernest wasn't very attentive as the service began. That day he felt like it was just something else his parents wanted him to do. That's when Pastor Graff started his sermon by asking the question, "WHAT ARE YOU BEING TEMPTED TO DO?"

Ernest sat up and looked right at Pastor Graff.

"What are you being tempted to do?" Pastor Graff repeated. Then he went on to talk about temptation. He talked about the devil luring us into actions and thoughts completely against what God would want—following our own desires and standards instead of His. He talked about being swallowed up by pride, about walking through life with attitudes that hurt others, and about disregarding any work of the Lord. He talked about doubting God's ability to make a difference in our lives. While Pastor Graff applied the issue of temptation to adults, to what they were going through, things like outright sins and disobedience, things like husbands and wives not caring for each other, unfaithfulness and bad attitudes at work, chasing after wealth, keeping God in church instead of walking with Him through the week—while Pastor Graff talked about those things, all Ernest could think about was his father's auger hidden in his closet.

Pastor Graff was preaching on the temptation of Jesus recorded in Matthew 4. After his summary of the tough temptations faced by the people of God in Harrison Town, Pastor Graff made another statement that caught Ernest's attention: *"Your temptation is tough, but Jesus is tougher."* Pastor Graff went on to read verse 4, where Jesus opposed the onslaught of the devil and said, "Man does not live on bread alone, but on every word that comes from the mouth of God." And he read verse 10, where Jesus said to the devil, "Away from me, Satan! For it is written: 'Worship the Lord your God, and serve Him only.' " Pastor Graff said that Jesus *stayed steady* under the assault of Satan. It was the season of Lent, a time to see Jesus as the one who keeps you steady in life. Jesus is the stabilizer. He broke the tempter's power when He gave His life on the cross, and He walks you through temptation with His forgiveness. He changes your outlook with His strength and presence. He is the one who gives you eternal life and who, by His love, calls you His friend. Pastor Graff quoted Hebrews 2:18, "Because [Jesus] Himself suffered when He was tempted, He is able to help those who are being tempted." Pastor Graff then asked the question, "Where do you need to stay steady?" He quoted 1 Corinthians 10:13 to close out the sermon: "No temptation has seized you except what is common to man. And God is faithful; He will not let you be tempted beyond what you can bear. But when you are tempted, He will also provide a way out so that you can stand up under it."

Ernest gulped. He was supposed to meet Paul Tucker at ten tomorrow morning, and he had his dad's auger in his closet. When Ernest left church there was a real battle going on inside of him. As his dad watched basketball that afternoon, Ernest sat on the couch next to him. "Dad," Ernest asked, "are you ever tempted?"

Ernest's dad was glad that Ernest heard some of the sermon. "I sure am."

"Like when?" Ernest asked.

"Well, I'm tempted to ignore my family when I watch these basketball games," Mr. Thorpe said as he turned off the TV. "I'm tempted not to appreciate my job and to complain about it. I'm tempted to be thoughtless to your mom instead of working to show my love. I'm tempted to worry about life and think I'm shouldering all the responsibility instead of trusting God. I'm tempted to use the bad language some of my co-workers use. There are many other times. I'm tempted to tell Uncle John to stop that old joke about the iron and steel business." Ernest and his dad laughed.

Mr. Thorpe continued, "What Pastor Graff said is true. Every day Jesus helps you through temptation. His Word reminds you over and over again. He gives you new strength and a new beginning. It works for me."

Evening came and Monday morning dawned. Mr. Thorpe was off to his job at the brooch factory. Mrs. Thorpe and Ernest's sister were going to the mall in Mount Pleasant. "What are you going to do today, Ernest?" they asked him.

"Nothing," Ernest replied.

Ten o'clock came and went. There was no phone call, no word. That evening at bedtime Mr. Thorpe went to kiss his son good-night. He sat on the bed for prayers. Then he asked, "What did you do today, Ernest?"

"Nothing, Dad."

Mr. Thorpe turned off the light, gave Ernest a kiss,

went over to the closet, and took out the auger. "Way to stay steady, Ernest. Good night."

How did he know?

It was a good start to Lent. Jesus was tougher, and He showed it in a vivid way for Ernest Thorpe through those boring but *steady* winter days in the heart of Michigan's vacationland.

LIVING
TRANSPARENTLY

· ·

Elsa Liebmann was one of the old folks in Harrison Town. She wasn't a vacationer or part of the old farm operations. She hadn't come to town years ago because of logging jobs. She was a pastor's wife. Her husband, the Reverend Frederick Martin, came to Harrison Town years ago to minister to a rough logging town. They had been through some tough but wonderful times. Pastor Martin's first call was to Alaska. Pastor and Elsa celebrated their first Christmas there. It was a special time. Elsa loved to recall those days.

Of course, Harrison Town was special too. But when Pastor Martin was only 55 years old, he died unexpectedly of a heart attack. Elsa stayed in Harrison Town. It was her home, and her family was close by. Years later she married Mr. Liebmann, a longtime friend of the family, who was a kind widower. They had a happy marriage, but a few years ago Mr. Liebmann died, and Elsa felt quite alone. She managed at home pretty well. Mid-Michigan Health Services helped her out as long as they could. Pastor Graff brought her Communion each month as it got tougher for her to get around. Finally she had to move. She was as sharp as a tack and had a way with words, but she just couldn't stay at home by herself. So she moved to Clare. The Clare/Gladwin Services for the Aging had a facility there—the Concord Center.

These facts are significant for two reasons. First, Mrs. Elsa Liebmann was Paul Tucker's grandma. Second, the seventh-grade teacher at the new middle school decided that each student would become a pen pal with a resident of the Concord Center in Clare. The teacher wanted those seventh graders to learn from and to show care for folks from a pre-Nintendo generation.

You couldn't pick one of your relatives, so Paul Tucker—this was before the auger incident—said to Ernest, "Hey, Ernest, my grandma is there! Pick her!" So Ernest did. Mrs. Elsa Liebmann was his new pen pal.

Ernest started writing right away. He introduced himself and asked all kinds of questions about Mrs. Liebmann. He received a prompt response. The first order of business, she said, was to call her Grandma Elsa. Being a friend of her grandson made him as close to family as you can get. Then she told Ernest all about her past. The letters were typed on an old manual typewriter. When Ernest found out that Grandma Elsa was a pastor's wife and that she knew Pastor Graff, he started sending her tapes of worship at St. Luke. Grandma Elsa always replied with cheerful letters. She told Ernest about life at the Concord Center: Bob Smith called and checked bingo; Florence Feigenbaum came home from the hospital; Mary Bessemer came to teach several of the ladies how to make various crafts; Jack and Janice Miller dropped by to take blood pressures. Then Grandma Elsa would comment about the sermon in a funny way. In one letter she wrote, "Pastor Graff says I should think about the hereafter. I do that a lot. Every time I go in my room I think, 'What am I here after?' " Once the sermon was about being precious in God's sight. Grandma Elsa wrote: "I surely am more precious the older I get. I've got lead in my feet, gas in my stomach, stones in my kidneys, gold in my teeth, and silver in my hair." Ernest really enjoyed Grandma Elsa's letters. That is, until he got this letter from her weeks after Christmas.

She wrote:

Dear Ernest,

With head hanging low in shame I am still trying to pick up the pieces. I was moved to the Concord Center without any help from me. There is so much missing from my old life. I loved being in Harrison Town and was much involved there for so many years. My new abode lacks no conveniences, and the folks living here are so anxious to be one's friend. Being a limping Lena I cannot participate in all their programs.

I apologize for not writing before Christmas. Thank you for your note. I live behind doors at the end of a long corridor (always carry six keys—security is tight) and a limping Lena no longer walks to the post office, so the delay. All our needs are taken care of here except rides to medical help, groceries, etc. Yesterday they told me this also means banking. So it is not perfect for someone such as old me, who never drove and had all this organized in Harrison Town. Grandpa Liebmann took such good care of me—he had time to spend with me, which Grandpa M hardly ever had, but that is how it is when you marry a preacher ... one walks alone. A blessed New Year to you.

Much love,
Grandma E.

When Ernest read that letter he was angry. Why would she send such a depressing letter? Grandma Elsa never used that tone before. How could she hurt him like that? This pen pal project was not very much fun anymore. Now what was he going to do? You see, Ernest was scheduled to meet Grandma Elsa in person next month. Now he wasn't looking forward to it. But he couldn't cancel it. The visit was part of the assignment.

Four weeks went by too quickly for Ernest. It was time to go to Clare. The school bus took the class down to the Concord Center. Ernest slunk into Grandma Elsa's little apartment and said hello. He sat on an olive green couch that looked pretty old. Grandma Elsa had a tough time getting Ernest to talk. Finally she said, "Ernest, what's wrong?"

Ernest looked at her and pulled out the last letter. He asked, "Why did you write such a sad note?" Grandma Elsa walked slowly to the couch and sat next to Ernest. Ernest could see that it wasn't easy for her to get around.

"I wrote a sad note because I was sad, Ernest," Grandma Elsa replied. She went on, "I thought you cared about me."

"I do care about you!" Ernest said.

"Do you care about me only when I'm feeling good?" Grandma Elsa asked.

Ernest mumbled, "Well ..."

Grandma Elsa went on: "Ernest, when you care about someone, it means that you care about their real inside self—happy or sad. You care about their problems and failures and fears. And you listen and help, if you can. Are you always happy and smiley and good for your parents, Ernest?"

Ernest mumbled again, "Well ..."

"You know, Ernest," Grandma Elsa said, "you sent me a tape of a sermon about a poor and miserable woman at a well. She wasn't very happy, and she wasn't the best of characters. But Jesus cared about her. He knew about her life. He knew she needed forgiveness, and He changed her life forever. Jesus cares about my inside self too. I can tell Him everything at anytime. He died for me. He's my Savior and my friend every day for my inside self. That's the kind of care you get, Ernest. And that's the kind of care you can show. One day I'll be with my dear ones in heaven, but now I need my dear ones on earth to show me the love of Jesus. I was being honest, Ernest. To God and to you too."

"But it doesn't always feel very good," Ernest said to Grandma Elsa.

"Well, that's true," she replied. "And that's a big problem of this generation. Being honest and caring doesn't feel good all the time, so people stop doing it. Maybe all of us need to stand face-to-face with Jesus at the well, Ernest! Sure it doesn't always feel good, but He's got what's good for us! He really cares, Ernest."

Grandma Elsa stopped herself. "Listen to me go on," she said. "I guess you got what you needed for your assignment—the opinion of another generation."

Everything Grandma Elsa said really got Ernest thinking. She could be feisty, but she was right. He never thought about caring about someone so much. He never realized how much Jesus cared for him. He visited with Grandma Elsa until it was time for the school bus to leave. He had a good time. She was a special lady, and it was frustrating for her to grow old. Not everybody remembered her inside self. As Ernest left he said, "I'll remember about being honest, Grandma Elsa."

"You do that, Ernest—especially after that *auger escapade* of yours!"

"How did you know about that?" Ernest asked in complete shock.

"Oh, that grandson of mine, Paul," she responded. "He can't keep a secret from me. I found out that Sunday before and called your dad right away. Didn't want a good pen pal like you to get suspended for life!"

"Thanks, Grandma Elsa," Ernest said.

He got on the bus. What an afternoon! But his pen pal report was no problem to write. Jesus and Grandma Elsa showed him what he learned. Ernest wrote: "I learned that being honest means there is really love there. And I learned that a real friend cares for your inside self." Then Ernest added, "And I learned to check in at the well more." Even if his teacher didn't get it, Ernest did.

BEING
UNCONVENTIONAL
● ●

In Harrison Town the unusual and unconventional stand out. You just can't blend in when the population
is so low and the inclination to spread the latest local
news via the phone or conversation at Ashcraft's Market
is so high. And there *are* the unconventional in Harrison
Town! Among Ernest Thorpe's legendary characters are
people like big Ron Hemmy. He was a legend on Budd
Lake for the time he jumped on a raft made out of 50-gal-
lon drums and lumber and broke it right in half. Then
there was Vern Flemming, who was known for wrecking
20 cars by the time he was 18 years old. The McCray
family was known as unconventional. Each year they
bought a brand new boat, and each year they tore the
propeller off that new boat by running into one obstacle
or another.

Even at St. Luke there were unconventional folks.
The most renowned had to be the custodian and sexton,
Mr. Staupzauge. He had the unfortunate habit of falling
asleep on the job. One Sunday this habit took control of

him during the Lord's Prayer. For 20 years he rang the little bell outside the church during the Lord's Prayer, but this Sunday he didn't do it. After church Pastor Graff asked Mr. Staupzauge how he could have missed ringing the bell during the Lord's Prayer. Mr. Staupzauge replied, "Pastor, if you were praying like you were supposed to, you never would have noticed!" Unconventional!

Another person who fell into the category of the unconventional was Ernest's mother. That's right, Mrs. Thorpe. That wasn't really discovered, however, until the year that the St. Patrick's Fair at St. Athanasius Church fell on a Sunday night. You've got to understand that everybody who was anybody in Harrison Town went to the St. Patrick's Fair at St. Athanasius Church. It was a big event with games and great prizes for the kids. There were crafts, good food, music, and plenty of conversation. It was one of the winter highlights in Harrison Town and a lot of fun for all the families involved.

After school one day, Ernest's friend Andy Oreby asked him, "Hey, Ernie, [you might remember that Andy Oreby was the only person who called Ernest *Ernie*] is your family going to the St. Patrick's Fair Sunday night?"

It was an innocent question, but as soon as Ernest heard the words *Sunday night* he panicked. Sunday night was reserved in the Thorpe household. Ernest knew that long before he was born his mom reserved Sunday night for being home, sitting quietly, and reading the Bible. It was her time. They didn't have to be in the room with her, but there was no TV or loud activity, just quiet time. Ernest's mom told him it was her time to get "sane" again. It had also become dependable family time in the

Thorpe home. So Ernest answered Andy, "I'll have to check."

Well, right away Andy pounced on Ernest for his hesitance. "What do you mean, check?" he asked. "Why *wouldn't* you go to the St. Patrick's Fair?"

Ernest replied quietly, "Well, Sunday night is my mom's quiet time, and I don't know if we'll go."

Saying those words to Andy Oreby was dangerous. Andy just happened to be a great adversary of the unconventional. Anyone who would do anything other than what he thought should be done was in danger of great scorn and criticism. So Andy piped up, "Well, that's pretty weird, Ernie! Have you heard that it's the 20th century?" he asked with a snide laugh. Ernest was usually laughing along with Andy Oreby about all the unconventional people they saw. But now Ernest was one of them. His family was in the category. While Andy continued to probe and laugh about the Thorpe family being hermits and buying an Amish horse and buggy, Ernest just walked away and made his way toward home.

It didn't take long for Mrs. Thorpe to see that Ernest was upset. When he walked in the door and didn't start rummaging around for food, Mrs. Thorpe followed him to his room and sat down with him. "What's wrong, Ernest?" she asked.

Ernest said, "Andy Oreby asked if we were going to the St. Patrick's Fair on Sunday night."

"Well, you can go with your friend," Mrs. Thorpe said.

Ernest was a little surprised. "But I told Andy it was your quiet time, and he laughed," Ernest replied.

"It's *my* quiet time, Ernest," his mother said. "I've enjoyed sharing it with you, but I knew the time would come when you might need to do other things."

"But," Ernest said, "Andy laughed at you."

Ernest's mom put her arm around him. "Ernest," she began, "a long time ago I began taking Sunday nights as my special time with the Lord. When my mother died, I needed that time to read the Bible and to pray. When I married your dad, he went along with that. And when I had you kids I *really* needed it more than ever! Ernest, I need what Jesus gives me during that special time. Not much is more important than that."

"Except when I spun off the living room chair and had to go to the emergency room," Ernest added.

"That's true, Ernest." They laughed a little bit.

Then Ernest asked, "Mom, what am I going to do about Andy?"

"Well, Ernest, maybe Andy's eyes aren't open," Mrs. Thorpe replied.

"What do you mean, Mom?"

"You know the story about Jesus healing the man who was blind. His neighbors thought he was crazy when he told about the good things Jesus did for him. The Pharisees decided to throw out of the synagogue anyone who believed that Jesus was the Savior. And they threw that man out when he said he was a follower of Jesus. But he knew what he knew. He knew Jesus had given him the help no one else could. He kept following the Lord. That's the kind of help Jesus has given me and you, Ernest. The fact is, it is no ordinary thing to believe in Jesus as your Savior, and it is no ordinary thing to live your Christian life. You just stand up to Andy, Ernest. Maybe you'll open his eyes."

The next morning in school Andy could hardly contain himself. "Hey Ernie, what about the St. Patrick's Fair?"

Ernest walked up to Andy Oreby, looked him straight in the eye, and said, "Andy, there's one thing I do know. I can go to that St. Patrick's Fair if I want to, but I'm staying home because what we do with God is important. And my mom is not weird! You can laugh all you want, but you're the one who's missing out!"

Ernest turned to walk away from a speechless Andy Oreby, but he quickly doubled back. "And Andy," he said, "my name is *Ernest*."

That was probably one of the most courageous things Ernest Thorpe had ever done. And all that week Andy Oreby was very quiet. Ernest stood up for what he knew was the undeniable truth. He stood up for his mom, for his family, for Jesus too. That was kind of scary to Ernest. He didn't know if Andy would ever talk to him again. He didn't know if Andy would talk *about* him to the other kids. But that really wasn't as important as it was a few days ago. Ernest never fully appreciated what his mom was all about. But under fire, his eyes were opened.

Sunday evening came and Mrs. Thorpe settled into her familiar chair in the family room. She read her Bible. Mr. Thorpe sat on the couch and read the paper. Ernest's sister played with her Barbie dolls in her room. And Ernest just sat, looking out the window. He was glad to be there. The silence was broken by a knock at the back door. Ernest opened the door and there was Andy Oreby.

"Hi, Andy," Ernest said.

Then Andy asked quietly, "Ernest, my mom said I could visit with you while they're at the St. Patrick's Fair. You busy?"

"No, come on in, Andy. We're having a good time."

The boys walked into the family room, sat down on the couch, and talked quietly about school and some new Nintendo games. Then they just sat and watched the snow fall. Ernest looked at his mom and smiled. Mrs. Thorpe knew she was not the only one with eyes opened that evening by the grace of God. And she wasn't the only one praying. No question about it—not one person that Sunday evening was unhappy to be in the ranks of the unconventional.

WANTING THE BEST

For Ernest, life at the new middle school was nice enough. The new facility on Main Street had everything a seventh grader needed for a good education. But for Ernest, and probably for most seventh graders, school was school. There were no great thrills in the Monday through Friday pursuits in the classroom.

That feeling was accentuated as spring made its way into the heart of Michigan's vacationland. The outdoors was beginning to tease every child who had been cooped up for the winter. The breezes from the south caused kids to unzip their heavy winter coats as they walked home from school. Hats and gloves were stashed in backpacks. Ernest even saw his first robin. Baseball season was close, and Ernest couldn't wait to sneak his Walkman to school so he could listen to the Detroit games during English class. School was school. Spring was calling. And the new middle school just didn't have the zip it had at the beginning of the year.

That outlook of Ernest Thorpe, however, changed quickly one day when Ernest's teacher had to have an emergency appendectomy. It was a shame. Ernest liked his teacher. He would be laid up for a little while, but he was okay. Then the principal, Mr. Black, introduced the substitute teacher. Her name was Miss Vanderveer. Ernest looked at her and froze. His mouth hung open. Suddenly any regrets about the confinement of school or the demanding work of the seventh grade left Ernest's mind. It was spring and he was looking at the most beautiful teacher he had ever seen. Ernest was in love!

He was also very quiet the rest of the day. Nothing could sway his attention from Miss Vanderveer's teaching expertise. And on the way home that day Ernest said nothing about baseball, Nintendo, or anything else. His friends thought something was definitely wrong. Through the week Ernest took an unusual interest in schoolwork. He raised his hand and asked questions like he had never done before. He inhaled with a deep breath every time Miss Vanderveer walked by his desk so he could smell her perfume. By the end of the week he had made a decision. Sure, Miss Vanderveer was old—probably at least 25—but she was the one he was going to marry.

As Ernest made decisions for his future, his family and friends wondered if he would live to see that future! Ernest was driving everyone crazy! He ignored his friends. He walked around in a daze at home. He started strategizing methods of impressing and winning the heart of Miss Vanderveer. Ernest wanted the best! That's just about when he found out about his parents' invitation.

At supper on Friday night, his mom said, "Ernest, I hear your teacher is doing very well down at the hospital in Clare. How do you like the substitute teacher?"

Ernest stopped chewing and stared straight ahead

with thoughts of wedding plans. Ernest's mom repeated, "Ernest!"

That broke his trance. He smiled and mumbled, "Oh, yeah."

Then his mom said, "With her being new to the school and all, we thought it would be nice to invite her to dinner. She's coming Sunday night."

Sunday night! In his own home! Miss Vanderveer! What was he going to do?

Ernest knew he had to impress her. He wanted to show her that he was the best! He was excused from the table and immediately went to check on what he had to wear. His Sunday shirt would be nice, but he didn't have a tie. Ernest looked in his dad's closet, but the few ties he had were too long and not impressive. Then Ernest spotted his sister's doll clothes in her room. One new dress was perfect. The size and pattern were just right. He walked into her room, grabbed the dress, snuck back into his room, and proceeded to cut a necktie out of the front of the dress! He was consumed with his mission and delighted with the finished product until his sister walked into his room and screamed!

That was the last straw for Ernest's parents. Their son was out of sorts all week. Now his sister was sobbing because he ruined one of her doll dresses. Mr. Thorpe called his mother and asked if Ernest could stay the night with her—perhaps do some hard labor at her house as well.

You might remember Emma Thorpe, Ernest's grandmother. She had 13 children and 42 grandchildren. No challenge was too great for her. After her volunteer work at the American Legion, she came to pick up Ernest.

"I hear you have a new necktie," she said to him as he got into the car. They drove to her house. Grandpa was ready with a bucket and a sponge. They were going to wash some walls. Ernest and his grandma started working, while Grandpa cleaned out the garage.

Emma Thorpe started the conversation. "Ernest, you're in love, aren't you?"

"What do you mean, Grandma?" Ernest replied quietly.

"Oh, I've seen it plenty of times. A boy doesn't go and make a necktie out of doll clothes just for the fun of it."

"But I want the best!" Ernest pleaded. "I want to look the best. Miss Vanderveer is the best, and I want her to know that I'm the one for her!"

"Ernest," Grandma said, "isn't she a little old for you?"

"She'll wait!" Ernest answered.

"Well, your grandpa didn't want me to wait," Emma said as she looked Ernest in the eye.

"What do you mean, Grandma?" Ernest asked.

"He didn't want me to wait. Your grandpa was going off to war. We wanted to be married, but he told me that if I found somebody, I should go ahead and settle down and be happy, because he might not come back."

"Didn't he love you, Grandma?"

"Ernest," Grandma replied, "he *did* love me! He wanted the best—but not for himself. He wanted the best for me. That's why I loved him. And that's why I waited. Ernest, you've got things a little backwards. If you're always wanting for yourself, you're never going to be happy. You're never going to be satisfied. But if you really want the best for others, then you'll know what love and being happy are all about."

Emma Thorpe put down her drying rag and walked over to a chair where her well-worn Bible lay. Ernest had seen that Bible plenty of times. His grandmother read it often and knew it well. As Ernest was growing up, it was from that Bible that his grandmother read Bible stories to him. She opened it up and read these words of Jesus spoken to disciples who were fighting for the best: "Whoever wants to become great among you must be your servant, and whoever wants to be first must be your slave—just as the Son of Man did not come to be served, but to serve, and to give His life as a ransom for many."

"Ernest," Grandma Thorpe said, "Jesus wanted the best, but not for Himself. He knew the best was what He could give. That's why He went to the cross to give His life to save you and me. And He is alive now to still give you and me His best! That's why I stick to this Bible. Jesus gives and helps and forgives, and that's the best!

"Ernest, if you really want to have the best, you might want to think hard not about what you can get, but about what you can give. What do you think is really the best for Miss Vanderveer?"

Ernest thought as he washed walls. He had made people pretty miserable the past few days. He was being selfish, and he knew love wasn't supposed to be that way. Ernest thought about being a servant. He knew Jesus was that for him. What would giving mean? What would be best for Miss Vanderveer? Ernest finally said,

"Well, Grandma, I suppose she shouldn't wait either."
Then he added, "But I sure wish I were 25!"

"You will be, Ernest," Grandma Thorpe replied,
"and I think you'll make someone very happy because
you'll know what it means to want the best."

Sunday evening came. It was almost time for supper. Ernest was in his room. The doorbell rang, and
Ernest could hear voices in the living room. He walked
in and his father said, "Ernest, I'd like you to say hello to
Miss Vanderveer and her fiancé. We asked him to join us
for dinner too."

Fiancé. Ernest smiled, walked up to the happy couple, held out his hand and said, "Congratulations." The
Thorpe family had a wonderful evening welcoming
their special guests. And Ernest knew it was the best.

DOING THE
AMAZING

Amazing things do happen! You've been hearing about some of the amazing events in Harrison Town, Michigan. And while it's true that day-to-day activity isn't all that amazing all the time, God's work in it sure is!

That truth applies to Harrison Town, Michigan, the beautiful small town in Michigan's heartland, nestled around the picturesque and slowly thawing Budd Lake. Life in a small town is really not all that amazing. Things probably get a little too routine in your life. Just think how routine things get in Harrison Town! For Pastor Graff and for many others in Harrison Town, however, the end of winter was anything but routine! Not just because of the Lenten countdown to Easter. No, this time of year brought the magic and wonder of high school basketball championship games! Pastor Graff loved basketball! And if you've ever been to Harrison Town and stopped in at St. Luke Lutheran Church, you know that the church is right next door to the high school. So not only was basketball a passion of Pastor Graff, it was also convenient! Pastor Graff peeked in on practices; he went to the games. He was an avid supporter of the Harrison Town Hornets. In fact, a member of St. Luke, Tim Farley, was on the team. So Pastor Graff had a close connection. The Harrison Town varsity team always did reasonably well but was never outstanding. The conference was tough. And funds for a full-blown varsity program were short, so the Hornets got by. Until a very special time.

The Harrison Town Hornets had gotten off to a great start, and they weren't letting up. They beat the Eagles of Farwell and the Houghton Lake Bobcats. They conquered Lake City, and the Clare Pioneers fell to their solid play. The Meridian Mustangs couldn't handle the Hornets' balanced attack. The Hornets were undefeated, but no headlines yet.

Through the basketball season and the Lenten season Pastor Graff kept up with his faithful work for the people of St. Luke. The excitement of basketball was always in the back of his mind too. One Sunday in Lent he preached on John 11, the chapter in the Bible where Lazarus was raised from the dead by Jesus. Pastor Graff's basic point in that Lenten sermon was this, when Jesus is at work, *the amazing takes place!* Pastor Graff spoke about Lazarus, the brother of Mary and Martha, a dear friend of Jesus. Lazarus was sick. But the disciples didn't want Jesus to go back to the area where Lazarus lived. There were many enemies there. Jesus decided to go, but Lazarus died before He arrived. Mary asked Him, "Why weren't you here?" And when Jesus saw where they had buried His friend, He wept. The shortest and one of the most comforting passages in Scripture, Pastor Graff noted, is "Jesus wept" (John 11:35). He shares our grief. Jesus asked that the stone be removed, but Martha said, "No, it's too late. It's too late."

Jesus persisted; the stone was removed; and He said, "Lazarus, come out!" And he did! Lazarus was alive! They even had to unwrap him! *Amazing!* Jesus brings life from death, joy out of sorrow! Pastor Graff noted that there were many individuals who wanted to stop Jesus. The Sanhedrin didn't believe that the *amazing* had any part in their lives. God's work didn't get involved like that, they said. Their negative and sinful outlook refused to let the amazing work of the Lord in.

With basketball on his mind Pastor Graff even worked in a Harrison Town Hornet illustration. Our tendency is to doubt, not to let God do His amazing work, Pastor Graff noted. Why, as the Harrison Town Hornets win games, as they stand undefeated, the most common outcry is, "It's just a matter of time. It won't go on." Who lets the amazing into their lives? But Pastor Graff closed out making the point that *when Jesus is at work, the amazing takes place!* His suffering and dying for us, His resurrection from the grave, His presence in Word and Sacrament, His help, His strength, His answer to our "*amazing*," Pastor Graff said.

Little did Pastor Graff know what was in store for the Hornets or for him in the next two weeks. The basketball team was still winning. The next game they played was for the Jackpine Conference championship. Now there were headlines. This was big! A week before the game, Tim Farley asked Pastor Graff to do the invocation for the big game—the Harrison Town Hornets versus the Beaverton Beavers. Everyone would be there! Pastor Graff was surprised by the request, but he said he would be honored. Wow. This would probably be the biggest crowd he ever spoke to. What would he say? He thought about it a lot that day. He talked to his wife about the opportunity. The next day he decided to stop by the high school to watch practice. In the hall on the way to the gym Pastor Graff met Mr. Barnes, the superintendent of the school. Mr. Barnes was a bold individual. He greeted Pastor Graff, patted him on the back, and said, "Well, Reverend, I hear you'll be doing the honors at the big game this weekend. Keep it short and sweet now! Heh, heh, heh!" Mr. Barnes laughed as he continued down the hall. The pressure was on. What could Pastor Graff say?

This opportunity was becoming a real burden. What could he say before a crowd interested in basketball? The next evening at confirmation class the topic of conversation among the kids was, of course, the big game against Beaverton. So Pastor Graff decided to ask his class, "What would you want to hear from me at the big game this weekend?"

Without a pause Ernest Thorpe, who was in the seventh-grade confirmation group, piped up and said, "Why don't you just tell everyone what you tell us? Why be any different?"

Pastor Graff stopped and smiled. "Thank you very much," he said to Ernest. "Thank you very much."

The night of the Jackpine Conference championship game came. The crowd packed the gym. The winner of this game would go to the state tournament. Superintendent Barnes walked onto the stage and hushed the crowd as he called for their attention. He welcomed everyone, spelled out some rules of conduct, then introduced Pastor Graff for the invocation.

Pastor Graff got up and walked toward the microphone. As he passed Mr. Barnes, Mr. Barnes winked at him and chuckled. Pastor Graff got to the microphone. All eyes were on him. He cleared his throat and began: "All of you are, no doubt, amazed at the success of your fine teams." The crowd broke into mild applause. It quieted down again. "This evening's game will bring more amazement," Pastor Graff went on to say. "It is my prayer that the thrill of this game will not be an empty thrill, but an opportunity to recognize Almighty God and His Son, who lives to do amazing work for us. *When Jesus is at work, the amazing takes place.* Jesus is at work today. We give Him thanks and begin in His name. Amen." Pastor Graff sat down. The crowd joined in singing the national anthem. Then the applause rumbled as the teams got ready to play.

The game began. The Hornets and Beavers were even from the opening jump ball. By halftime the gym had heated up with the sweat of the players and perspiration of the spectators. The score was 32–32. The Beavers came out strong in the second half. They pulled away by nine early. Harrison Town had to battle back, and battle they did. They closed the gap, but time was running out. There were 30 seconds left. Beaverton hit a clutch jumper to take the lead 63–62. Harrison Town took the ball out, and the Beavers pressured all the way. Steve Hartman dribbled around the left side, pulled up for a three-pointer, and missed! But he was fouled! That meant three free throws. The crowd was hushed. Beaverton's coach called a time-out. When the officials were ready, Hartman walked up to the free-throw line. There were 17 seconds left. The first free throw went up and in! Then the second and the third! The Hornets hit three free throws! They were up 65–63. Harrison Town called a time out to strategize defense. The Beavers put the ball into play. Harrison Town put some pressure on. The clock was ticking down. The Beavers got it across half court when Tim Farley intercepted a slow Beaverton pass! He took the ball down court for the lay-up and was fouled! Eight seconds left! Farley hit the first. Then the second. The score was now 67–63 Harrison Town. The crowd was going wild. Harrison Town put some pressure on for the inbound. The ball went into play. The clock ran. A Beaverton player went for a three-pointer and hit it, and the buzzer sounded! The final score was 67–66! The Harrison Town Hornets were conference champs! It was amazing! *Amazing!*

All through the crowd came the word *amazing!* Mr. Barnes turned to Pastor Graff and exclaimed, "That was an *amazing* game, Reverend!"

"It sure was," Pastor Graff replied with a big wink of his eye.

Amazing. Mr. Barnes remembered. So did many others, including Ernest Thorpe, who sat in the crowd with his family. This was basketball, but there was something else. It was *amazing.* How wonderful that the Savior could bring an amazing thrill to a high school gymnasium, and He wouldn't stop there.

LISTENING
CAREFULLY

A good story. That was what Enest Thorpe was after as he reached the home stretch of his seventh-grade year. His teacher was back after his emergency appendectomy, and one of the first assignments to the class involved current events. Each student was to find the most important news item they could in town and write a brief report on it. The news items would be printed in a seventh-grade headline book for them to keep for posterity. The person who came up with the most dynamic and meaningful item would get front-page coverage—complete with byline—in the headline book. Competition was great incentive for the seventh-grade class. The assignment was due next week Monday. The news hunt was on!

Ernest Thorpe decided to devise his own plan of action. In fact, every student devised his or her own plan of action! No one wanted to reveal what scoop they might get—and with it the front-page story and byline in the headline book!

After school each day Ernest searched for news. His first point of attack: the newspaper! Hmmm. The front page had blockbusters like this: "Fire Chief urges home-owners to keep chimneys clean." No, not enough zip, Ernest thought. The "Clare 1993 Pipfest" was coming up. What's a "Pipfest"? No, not that. "Two-car crash injures three." Not unique enough.

Ernest looked through the engagements, the birth announcements, and the classified ads. He saw the big news that the dental hygienist was visiting Hillside Grade School. Ken's Party Store was going to have the town's first public fax machine. Perhaps the newspaper wasn't the way to go.

Fortunately, it was only Monday night. There was plenty of time for new strategies. As Ernest lay in bed that night he thought and thought. Where can I get a big story? How can I find the big news? Then it hit him! He had to *find* it! A roving reporter is what he had to be! He decided to hunt around town each day after school for the big, breaking news stories that Harrison Town was ready to deliver.

On Tuesday after school Ernest decided to begin his roving reporter expeditions by visiting the hub of all Harrison Town activity—the Chamber of Commerce. The big story there? Christmas in July Craft Show booth space was still available. That was it. Well, there were plenty of other news items in town. Ernest would not be defeated! He stopped by the American Legion Hall. The Spring Polka Party was coming up. Okay, what about environmental issues? That would have to be on the cutting edge of major news! Perhaps an extinct species of fish in Budd Lake? Maybe illegal toxic-waste dumping in town? Ernest went to the Department of Natural Resources office. The waterfowl hunting stamp design contest was on. Nothing else. Another dead end. How about human-interest stories? People's lives! Heart-wrenching tales of human tragedy! The deep dark secrets and scandals in Harrison Town! Ernest went to the barbershop, sat in the waiting area with his face in a comic book, and he listened. He must have read that comic book five times and all he heard was that a sermon shouldn't be any longer than 10 minutes and the new dump shouldn't be located so close to town.

Well, it was Friday already. Ernest hadn't come up with anything! All he found out was that there were too many things going on in the world, and not a lot of it mattered. There were also too many things going on in the world that weren't doing people much good. What could Ernest write? What was the most important news item in Harrison Town? Saturday came, then Sunday. The assignment was due tomorrow. Ernest's mind was full and swirling. What could he write?

In that state of mind, after a frustrating week, Ernest accompanied his family to church. Ernest was worried and worn out. He couldn't focus on anything that morning. All he knew was that Pastor Graff had a long Bible reading. As Ernest closed his eyes, wiggled around, and bobbed his head, Mr. Thorpe took a look at the sorry state of his son and jabbed him in the ribs with an elbow. "Straighten up and listen," Mr. Thorpe whispered firmly into Ernest's ear. Ouch! Ernest sat up straight, listened to Pastor Graff, and heard these words from Matthew:

> From the sixth hour until the ninth hour darkness came over all the land. About the ninth hour Jesus cried out in a loud voice, *"Eloi, Eloi, lama sabachthani?"*—which means, "My God, My God, why have You forsaken Me?"

> When some of those standing there heard this, they said, "He's calling Elijah."

> Immediately one of them ran and got a sponge. He filled it with wine vinegar, put it on a stick, and offered it to Jesus to drink. The rest said, "Now leave Him alone. Let's see if Elijah comes to save Him."

> And when Jesus had cried out again in a loud voice, He gave up His spirit.

> At that moment the curtain of the temple was torn in two from top to bottom. The earth shook and the rocks split. The tombs broke open and the bodies of many holy people who had died were raised to life. They came out of the tombs, and after Jesus' resurrection they went into the holy city and appeared to many people.

> When the centurion and those with him who were guarding Jesus saw the earthquake and all that had happened, they were terrified, and exclaimed, "Surely He was the Son of God!"

Pastor Graff preached about Jesus' crucifixion and death that day. What caught Ernest's ear was that Pastor

Graff called it *good news!* Sins taken away. The hurt of humanity and the world carried to the cross through death to life. Hope and a new beginning through God's gracious work in Jesus. Pastor Graff said that when Jesus plunged into death, it shook death up so much that even believers who were dead were raised to life. The hopelessness and stranglehold were broken. *Good news!*

As Ernest heard all that, he thought, Hey! Hey! I've been on the wrong track! I've been listening to the wrong things! This has *got* to be the most important news in Harrison Town! *Good news!*

Ernest was fired up. After church he said, "Mom, Dad, I know what I'm going to write for my report. I know the most important news item in Harrison Town. Just wait till you see it!"

The Thorpes got home, ate lunch, and Ernest went to work. He wrote, "The most meaningful news item in Harrison Town that really affects people's lives is not found in the whole bunch of little things going on every day. I found plenty of that kind of news. There were activities, contests, accidents, and events. All of it keeps everybody very busy, but it really doesn't change anyone's life. The news that really makes a difference in how people feel and in life is what I found on Sunday morning." Then Ernest wrote out in newspaper-column style the verses he heard Pastor Graff read that morning. At the bottom of his news report he wrote, "The most important news is that Jesus is our Savior! It's *good news!*" Ernest put his report in a yellow folder with a clear cover to make it look good. Wow! His report was finished! He found the news in a place that he didn't expect. Now he was ready to turn in his assignment.

The kids couldn't wait to find out who would get the front-page spot in the headline book. Ernest's teacher said he would return the projects by Wednesday, and by Friday the headline book would be ready for printing. Ernest really felt like he had a unique news item and the best one.

Wednesday morning came, and his teacher handed back the news reports. Ernest opened his up and this is the comment he read, "Ernest, I appreciate your reporting, but we can't print this. Please find another item for the headline book." Ernest couldn't believe it. His teacher announced that the front-page article would be the story by Charmaine Gunderson on the reopening of Bucilli's Pizza and Family Restaurant.

Ernest was silent. During lunch he took his report to his teacher. "This is a headline story!" Ernest said. "I think this is the most important news in Harrison Town!"

"I'm sorry, Ernest," his teacher replied. "You did nice work, but you'll just have to find another story for the headline book."

So it was, that the way of faith, passion, and the cross in a boy's life in Harrison Town, Michigan, did not make the headlines. Would that be the end? Would the town miss out on hearing the most important news? With Ernest around I wouldn't bet on it.

III

STORIES OF A COMEBACK

NEVER A DOUBT!

"Comebacks are now the name of the game." I read that headline in *USA Today*. The sports columnist noted that all the recent attention-getters in sports were comeback figures. I happened to be reading that comeback article while enjoying a comeback myself. I was sitting on a porch overlooking Budd Lake. It was our comeback vacation in Michigan's heartland. 20 LAKES IN 20 MINUTES, the license-plate frame said. A NUMBER 1 AMERICAN CITY IN MICHIGAN'S VACATIONLAND. Paul Harvey's news reports and National Weather Service updates are the big radio attractions. Road construction stretched 1 MILES, as the sign said, as Main Street in Harrison Town was resurfaced. It was finished in a day. Wilson State Park was full, fire danger was low, but the big news during that year's comeback to Harrison Town was the anniversary celebration at St. Luke.

The official church was 20 years old. Ministry had been going on for some time in Harrison Town. It started with the logging industry and all the workers who moved up there. Then it continued as a summer preaching station for the Lutherans who spent their summers in the woods and on the lakes of the area. But in 1973, St. Luke Lutheran Church became an official congregation.

There were big plans for the anniversary. A special banner was being made. Bookmarks would also commemorate the occasion. There was a publicity committee, a food-planning committee, an invitation committee. A group was writing the official church history. There was a lot of excitement and plenty of work to be done.

The Thorpe family was, of course, quite involved in the anniversary plans. Mr. Thorpe was helping with setup. Mrs. Thorpe had plenty of baking to do. But Ernest wasn't quite yet switched into the work mode. So Mrs. Thorpe, trying to stem the tide of summer boredom and/or mischief, decided to volunteer her son for a special task. It was the *St. Luke Lutheran 20th Anniversary Ad Book.* Businesses and organizations had to be approached and asked to purchase an ad so that they could show support for the church that had shared 20 years of life in Harrison Town. Legwork was needed, and Ernest was volunteered. He wasn't thrilled about the task. After all, it was summer. He had important things to do: blaze new trails in the woods; swim to new depths in Budd Lake for example. But Ernest's mom told him those things could wait until after the noon siren. He could do the ad book in the morning instead of lying in bed.

The decision was made. After church one Sunday Pastor Graff gave Ernest a quick training course. He was supposed to say, "Hi, my name is Ernest Thorpe, and I'm from St. Luke Lutheran Church. I'm here to ask if you would like to offer your support and congratulations for our 20th anniversary by purchasing an ad in our ad book.

Please take a look at what we have so far." Then he was supposed to hand the book to the person, let him or her look at it, and be sure to get a business card and payment if the person said yes. All funds would go to the John Paul Memorial Parking Lot and Mission Outreach Fund.

Ernest didn't want to do it. Why should he have to spend his summer mornings trudging around town? What good could an anniversary ad book do anyway? Besides, he was not thrilled about talking to a bunch of people he didn't know, and he wasn't even getting paid! This was not the way he would have his summer go. His parents, however, did not share Ernest's sentiments. And despite last-minute efforts by Ernest to win a reprieve—offers to do the dishes for life and to wash the truck every week were a couple of his tactics—Ernest found himself up bright and early Monday morning, pedaling his bicycle to the IGA for his first ad book request.

Most local folks shopped at the IGA. Ashcraft's Market was pretty touristy. So the manager of the IGA knew Ernest's parents. Well, Ernest did as Pastor Graff had instructed: "Hi, my name is Ernest Thorpe, and I'm from St. Luke Lutheran Church. I'm here to ask if you would like to offer your support and congratulations for our 20th anniversary by purchasing an ad in our ad book. Please take a look at what we have so far." He handed the book to the manager, let him look at it, and told him that all funds would go to the John Paul Memorial Parking Lot and Mission Outreach Fund.

Ernest did not show a lot of enthusiasm. But was Ernest surprised at the response! The manager looked at the ad book. He looked at Ernest. Then he looked at that ad book again. And with a big smile and a firm handshake he said, "Young man, I'd be proud to have an ad in this book." He gave Ernest a check and a business card and said, "You keep up the good work!" It went a lot better than Ernest thought it would.

Ernest went across the street to the *Clare County Cleaver* to give it another try. Another firm handshake, another word of encouragement, and another donation came his way. Ernest worked his way down Main Street until the noon siren sounded. At every stop he was well received. Not everyone gave a donation, but there was always a word of encouragement and statements such as, "I'm behind you 100 percent. You're right on target. This sure is refreshing!"

That evening, Ernest let his parents know about his success, and he was fired up. It didn't take him long to spring out of bed each morning after that, and he ended up saturating the city with the ad book. There wasn't a business owner who didn't get a good look at it. From the Remedy Restaurant and Lake View Motel on one side of town to the Dairy Queen and Monte's Italian Restaurant on the other, everybody saw that book. Some even made a copy of the front page to post in their establishment.

On Saturday night Ernest reflected on his successful ad-book campaign. As Ernest spoke of his great sales ability, his smooth manner of speech, and his power of persuasion, his mom said to him, "Ernest, did you read the front page of the book yet?" No, Ernest hadn't. He was too involved in getting ads and enjoying his success. His mom told him, "Why don't you take a look?"

Ernest opened the book to the page everyone turned to when they considered an ad. He expected to find samples that got everyone else to jump on the band-wagon. Instead, there was an introduction letter from Pastor Graff along with something that looked very familiar. This is what Ernest read:

Dear Friend of St. Luke Lutheran,

It's a great blessing to celebrate an anniversary. But we're not just celebrating a span of time. We are celebrating the great way of God for us over these 20 years. We are celebrating His grace that has touched the lives of people in Harrison Town and around the world. One of our own young people, Ernest Thorpe, wrote about this grace of God for his seventh-grade headline book last year. His article was never published. But I think it is an appropriate summary of our 20 years of ministry here in Harrison Town and deserves prominent display for the members of our community.

Then came Ernest's article from last year!

The most meaningful news item in Harrison Town that really affects people's lives is not found in the whole bunch of little things going on every day. I found plenty of that kind of news. There were activities, contests, accidents, and events. All of it keeps everybody very busy, but it really doesn't change anyone's life. The news that really makes a difference in how people feel and in life is what I found on Sunday morning: *From the sixth hour until the ninth hour darkness came over all the land. About the ninth hour Jesus cried out in a loud*

voice, ... "My God, My God, why have You forsak-
en Me?" ... And when Jesus had cried out again in
a loud voice, He gave up His spirit. ... When the
centurion and those with him who were guarding
Jesus saw the earthquake and all that had happened,
they were terrified, and exclaimed, "Surely He was
the Son of God!" (Matthew 27:45–54). The most
important news is that Jesus is our Savior! It's
good news!

Ernest was amazed when he read that. That's why
there was so much support! That's why all the encouragement came his way. He thought his article was gone for
good, but now the whole town had read about the most
important news in Harrison Town. What an amazing
comeback! What a great way God chose to get His Word of
grace out. What great news for Ernest to know that his
seventh-grade disappointment was taken care of by God
in a wonderful way! Should he have ever doubted?

On Sunday the following week the St. Luke
anniversary celebration took place. The sanctuary was
crowded for the worship service. Pastor Graff preached
on Elijah in 1 Kings 19. He noted that over the 20 years of
St. Luke's existence there had been both ups and downs.
For members of that congregation there had been good
times and hard times. And while complaints and questions and feelings of hopelessness might be the first reaction—just like Elijah—the gracious way of God can
always be trusted. Even through adversity the Lord
didn't let Elijah down. There were 7,000 still faithful.
Even through the burden of sin and grief and death the
Lord didn't let us down. There was Jesus on the cross for
us. Even through what might come in the next 20 years

of life at St. Luke, God's way of grace and everlasting life will not stop. It might not be the way each person would choose, but there is never a doubt when it comes to the faithfulness and love and outreach of our Lord Jesus, who gave us life!

It rained at the anniversary picnic that afternoon. But that Sunday evening Ernest was still amazed at how God had worked a blessing out of what seemed pretty hopeless. Mrs. Thorpe sat down during her quiet time, gently tore the front page from the ad book, and placed it in her Bible. She was proud, but most of all God had given her another reason to say, "Never a doubt, Lord. Never a doubt."

WORTH IT!

* *

Summer vacation is always a special time. Having some time off makes it possible to step back and see more of the big picture of what life and faith are all about. Of course, the big picture is not always very easy to see. You and I get caught up in the calendar-packing activities of life—the pressure, tension, and demands, and pretty soon it's hard even to see tomorrow! You might feel that way right now. In Harrison Town, where Budd Lake shimmers in the moonlight and dances with the summer breeze, Ernest Thorpe had a hard time seeing the big picture too.

Many people who knew Ernest knew that he was a responsible boy. Whenever something went wrong, they suspected Ernest was responsible. Ernest Thorpe almost lived down to that reputation when the big picture slowly slipped from his view following St. Luke's 20th anniversary.

You see, Paul Tucker, his classmate of many grade-school years and his near-partner in augering out the middle school principal's ice-fishing shanty last winter, was hatching another plot. Ernest tried to keep his distance from Paul Tucker through the school year, but now it was summer, and Paul wasn't so bad as long as there were trails to ride bikes on and fish to catch. Paul had heard about Ernest's article being printed in the anniversary ad book. A lot of people had heard about it, and when Paul and Ernest stopped at McDonald's for a coke on a warm Saturday afternoon, Paul couldn't help but get in a dig at their seventh-grade teacher.

"You sure showed him, Ernest," Paul said. "I can't believe he didn't print that. He didn't treat you right." Ernest sipped his coke and just looked at Paul. "Yep," Paul said, "you must really be bad news in his eyes. I bet he told everyone that your article wasn't fit to print. You probably have a bad reputation with the teachers now."

Ernest couldn't believe what he was hearing. Surely he wouldn't have a bad reputation because of that article. Of course, it didn't get printed. Maybe he did get a bad deal after all! Maybe his teachers would make it extra hard for him this year! His seventh-grade teacher *was* unfair! What would stop him from going further?

Then Paul went on, "You've got to fight back, Ernest. I'll tell you what. I'll help you egg his house. Yep, I'll stand up for your rights! Tomorrow at sunset I'll egg his house good. I'll let you know how it goes." Paul said good-bye, climbed on his bike, and rode off.

Ernest felt angry that he had been treated unfairly. He was glad Paul was going to set things straight. His teacher deserved it.

There was adventure in the air for Ernest as he went to sleep that night. Morning came, and it was off to church. It was a typical Sunday morning. He saw familiar faces. He peeked in the kitchen to check out the cookies for later, then he started to make his way to his family's spot when he saw someone he hadn't planned on seeing. Could it be? It was! His seventh-grade teacher was at church, and he was walking toward him! Ernest froze. He smiled and said hello in a weak and guilty voice. His teacher said, "Hello, Ernest! I just had to come and visit your church. I saw the ad book, and I was so happy Pastor Graff decided to put it in. When I gave your article to him I explained the circumstances about the public school publications, but I was sure he would be proud of what you wrote."

Ernest's eyes were wide open with shock. "Y-y-you gave it to Pastor Graff? Why?" Ernest asked.

His teacher replied, "Ernest, I'm a Christian too. I really believe what you wrote. Besides, you're worth it. You're worth it."

Uh-oh. All Ernest could think about was sunset and Paul Tucker and eggs. His mom wanted to go to the American Legion Hall for brunch after church, but Ernest said he didn't feel well. Scrambled eggs was *not* a sight he wanted to see. He *had* to get in touch with Paul Tucker before sunset! He tried calling that afternoon. No answer. He called four more times. Still no answer. Ernest knew there was only one way out. He had to intercept Paul at home or at his teacher's house. And to do that, he had to confess to his parents!

It was crunch time. Ernest walked into the family room and told his parents the whole story. His dad sprang into action. "Ernest, get into the truck." Off they drove toward Paul Tucker's house. Paul wasn't there. His older sister said he went for a bike ride. Mr. Thorpe headed toward Lake Street, where Ernest's teacher lived. As they turned onto Lake, Ernest spotted Paul. Mr. Thorpe stopped the truck, stopped Paul, and said, "Paul, I think you better ride with us." Ernest told Paul what had happened. Ernest's father told Paul that he would be calling his parents. And Ernest was very quiet as he drove home with his dad at sunset.

Ernest knew he was wrong. He accepted the fact that Budd Lake was off-limits for the week and he was grounded because of this egg escapade. He was truly sorry. He could tell his parents were very disappointed. Before he went to bed Ernest asked, "Mom and Dad, how can you put up with me when I do stuff like this?"

His mother answered, "Ernest, we love you. God gave you to us. You're worth it."

There it was again. Worth it. There was a message in there somewhere. That week Wednesday, at Wednesday school at church—there was no room for Sunday school on Sunday mornings—Ernest heard those words again. Pastor Graff was talking to junior high students about self-esteem. "There was a Canaanite woman," Pastor Graff said. "Her daughter suffered from demon possession, and this woman had heard about Jesus. She knew God's plan to reach the people of Israel first. She knew she didn't deserve anything from Jesus. But she also knew God's promise to reach out with His mercy to the world. So she approached Jesus. Even though the disciples wanted to shoo her away, Jesus' love and mercy and care were there for her. And He healed her daughter." Pastor Graff went on to have a self-esteem discussion with the class. There were only three kids, and Ernest didn't say too much, so it wasn't much of a discussion, but Ernest got the message. Pastor Graff read a slew of verses from the Bible: "I have loved you with an everlasting love" (Jeremiah 31:3); "This is what the Lord says—He who created you … He who formed you … 'Fear not, for I have redeemed you; I have summoned

85

you by name; you are Mine' " (Isaiah 43:1); "Never will I leave you; never will I forsake you" (Hebrews 13:5); "I am the good shepherd. The good shepherd lays down His life for the sheep" (Jesus' words in John 10:11); "This is how God showed His love among us: He sent His one and only Son into the world that we might live through Him. This is love: not that we loved God, but that He loved us and sent His Son as an atoning sacrifice for our sins" (1 John 4:9–10). The message was clear. Nothing we do gives us worth. We are "worth it" because of Jesus' redeeming love for us. Pastor Graff said the love of God would never change. He still comes to us through the Bible and through Baptism and Communion with forgiveness and the news of life everlasting and says, "You're worth it because I love you."

That's what Ernest heard from his parents and his seventh-grade teacher too. It was true. Paul Tucker and a lot of other things made him doubt that. But if God says you're worth it, Ernest thought, then it's got to be true. And it really makes a difference in your life.

As my wife and I sat in church at St. Luke, watching our girls squiggle and squirm, the message was clear too. They're worth it. And what a privilege to know that our Father in heaven looks at us in the same way: *worth it, loved, forgiven.*

Budd Lake still shimmered in the moonlight and danced with the summer breeze. And whether it's just another day in Harrison Town or just another soon-to-be eighth-grade boy or an extraordinary act of God in life, the message *is* clear: In your life, through it all, comes the love and grace of God to lift you up, to give you the big picture, and to say, "You're *worth it!*"

STRETCHING OUT!

· ·

Harrison Town is surrounded by some great things! Beautiful pine forests stand tall. Lakes are clear and cool. Stars fill the sky each clear evening. Those wonderful surroundings, however, are not of primary interest to the people of Harrison Town, especially when the Clare County Fair gets into full swing!

For Ernest Thorpe, fresh-baked elephant ears, carnival rides, and the four-wheel-drive mud bog competition beat out pristine pine forests any day! The 110th Annual Clare County Fair was a big event! Everybody got involved. The Congregational Church was back with their delicious goulash suppers. The 4-H'ers sold hot dogs two for a dollar to give the Congregational ladies some competition. Hundreds of people entered baked goods and crafts with the hopes of winning a blue ribbon and a cash prize. All the concerts were sold out for the week. Tanya Tucker, Kenny Rogers, and the Oak Ridge Boys were the big-name performers. There was even a shuttle service from the parking lot to the midway. Someone had welded a bunch of metal chairs to a flatbed and hooked it up to a tractor.

Unfortunately, all the news from the fair wasn't good. On the first evening two people were injured on the octopus ride. Apparently a cotter pin came loose and caused a mother and her son to be bounced around a bit too much. They were treated and released at the Clare hospital. Everyone was thankful that it wasn't more serious, but with the headline article in the *Clare County Cleaver* and the talk that took place around town, people were being extra cautious with fair rides.

As you might imagine, Ernest's timing to talk his sister into trying the rides was not very good. She was four going on five. Karen had never been a big fan of fair rides. Oh, she had tried a few: the kiddy train and the merry-go-round. But those were about the limit. In fact, this octopus incident convinced her that fair rides were out of the question. Ernest, however, wouldn't stand for that kind of behavior. His sister was not going to be afraid of fair rides! What would people say? So he started his campaign.

He started out nice enough, offering to buy her a wristband on kids' day. She could go on all the rides she wanted! And she didn't have to worry because she was too small for some of those fast ones anyway! No deal. His sister wouldn't budge. After more bribery with cotton candy, elephant ears, and candy worms fell through, Ernest got a little more intense. Her friend Missy wasn't afraid of the rides. Why was she? This new tactic got underway, but Ernest's sister was saved by a call to supper. Ernest just looked at his sister during the meal. This had become a case of will against will.

Family devotions followed supper. Mr. Thorpe read from a Bible storybook. Both Ernest and his sister enjoyed hearing the accounts from the Bible. They were on Exodus and God setting His people free from Pharaoh. Mr. Thorpe read,

> God also said to Moses, … "I have heard the groaning of the Israelites, whom the Egyptians are enslaving, and I have remembered My covenant. Therefore, say to the Israelites: 'I am the Lord, and I will bring you out from under the yoke of the Egyptians. I will free you from being slaves to them, and I will redeem you with an outstretched arm and with mighty acts of judgment. I will take you as My own people, and I will be your God, … who brought you out from under the yoke of the Egyptians.' "

Mr. Thorpe read about how God saved His people, how it was an amazing change of life and relief of a great burden for them. The Bible storybook pointed out that Jesus saved us too, from the sin and hurt and death in our lives that sometimes feel worse than slavery. The Thorpe family closed with a prayer of thanks for God's outstretched arm of salvation in Jesus. Ernest listened, but he wasn't paying close attention. He was more interested in getting his sister on those rides.

The next afternoon opportunity came knocking. Ernest and his sister went to the fair. She couldn't pass up the fresh-made fudge he promised her. While they were there, Ernest saw Missy with her mom.

"Hello, Missy," Ernest said. "How would you like to go on a ride with my sister? I've got four tickets here in my pocket—just enough to let each of you have a turn on the *dragon ride.*" The dragon ride was a roller coaster for little kids. It was in the shape of a purple dragon and went in a loop of quick ups and downs. After several times around, it switched directions and made several more loops backwards!

"Thank you, Ernest!" Missy said. Then she asked Ernest's sister to go with her. Ernest was beaming when his sister agreed—reluctantly.

The first part of the ride wasn't too bad. Ernest saw his sister smiling and laughing as the purple dragon went around and around. But then came the backwards part. Ernest saw his sister's face change quickly. As soon as the dragon jerked backwards, her eyes opened wide with fear. She began to cry and then to scream. She was scared! Ernest felt helpless as he watched his sister go round and round. He didn't know what to do. That's when he saw the man who operated the ride spring to his feet and push the stop button. The man guided the purple dragon to a halt, unbuckled Ernest's sister's safety belt, and stretched out his arms to lift her out of her seat. He calmed her down and carried her down the stairs to Ernest. The man put Ernest's sister down, wiped away her last tear, and said, "Take good care of her now."

Ernest walked her over to a bench. They both sat down. Ernest gave her a big hug and said, "I'm sorry, Karen." As they sat there together, Ernest thought how thankful he was for that man who cared enough to help his sister. And when the image of the man's outstretched arms went through his mind, Ernest remembered what his dad read the night before. When he saw his sister's face change from terrible fear to relief, and when he looked at her now, he understood what it meant to be saved.

That evening at family devotions Ernest's father read the next part of Exodus from the Bible storybook. It was about Moses, the plagues, and the crossing of the Red Sea. Ernest had seen *The Ten Commandments,* so he had a vivid picture of the crossing of the Red Sea and the rescue of the people of Israel. That Bible story closed with a verse from Isaiah 43 as the book spoke of our living Savior and His rescue of us:

> Fear not, for I have redeemed you; I have summoned you by name; you are Mine. When you pass through the waters, I will be with you; and when you pass through the rivers, they will not sweep over you. When you walk through the fire, you will not be burned; the flames will not set you ablaze. For I am the LORD, your God, the Holy One of Israel, your Savior.

As the book went on to talk about forgiveness of sins and eternal life through Jesus' death on the cross and His presence and help through all of life, Ernest thought about the dragon ride, his life, and how thankful he was for a Savior with outstretched arms.

Ernest was also thinking about Karen, his little sister. Ernest realized that he was thinking only of himself. He was not being caring, and it was about time he started *stretching out* a little himself. It was the least he could do: to show compassion and love and to start where it was most difficult—right at home.

So it was that the outstretched arms of Jesus continued to reach into the lives of the Thorpe family in Harrison Town. As Cindy and I and the girls packed up to head home and to start work and kindergarten and potty training, there was no doubt about the out-stretched arms of the Lord who had refreshed us on our vacation comeback. Through His saving and strengthening Word and Sacrament, there is no doubt about the outstretched arms of the Lord for you. Isn't it great to know that the salvation of the Lord through Jesus in your life and your stretching out to show His real care and compassion to the people in your life isn't just a story!

IV

STORIES OF EXPECTATION

LOOKING OUT

It was a few days before Thanksgiving. The big news was not the Thanksgiving doings lined up for the long weekend. The news was the *forecast*. The *weather* forecast. Everyone in Harrison Town expected snow around Thanksgiving time. But Paul Weatherhead, the local radio weatherman, was predicting more than flurries! As the week went on the weather predictors warned residents of north-central Michigan that a blizzard could be on its way. A heavy system of precipitation was moving in from the northwest. Once it crossed Lake Michigan it was expected to intensify, stall, and bring heavy snow! The expected time of arrival was Saturday night.

This was exciting! The whole town reacted. The Harrison Town schools checked their school-cancellation procedure—which radio station to call and which phone calls to make. Harrison Town Lumber and Hardware made sure its supply of snow shovels was on display and ready to sell. The mechanic at the Amoco station was swamped with snow blowers to recondition and four-wheel-drive vehicles to winterize. The IGA and Ashcraft's Market were selling milk and bread and other essentials faster than they could keep the shelves stocked. Ernest Thorpe, now in the heart of his eighth-grade year, and his friends were filled with the excitement of possible days off from school, revenue from snow-shoveling jobs, and fun from rides in their families' snowmobiles!

The town buzzed with excitement. Pastor Graff wondered whether or not he would have to cancel church because of the "blizzard of the century." At the Thanksgiving Day worship service, he told the folks they shouldn't take any chances if the snow did come Saturday night.

Well, Saturday came. You could see the anticipation on everyone's face as you walked through town. Ernest and his dad got home that evening after running a few errands. Ernest could even see the excitement in his dad's eyes as he listened to the radio and heard the forecast of the big snow.

Flurries started to fall as Ernest and Karen went to bed that night. They looked forward to a thick blanket of snow the next morning. Finally morning came. Ernest jumped out of bed, looked out the window—and didn't see anything. No snow! Nothing! They were wrong. They were wrong!

The Thorpe family got ready for church. It was more quiet than usual as they ate breakfast and headed off to St. Luke's. Some of the folks at church were joking about the weather people and another false alarm. But it was clear that Ernest was not the only one who was disappointed. Church began. Things were a little lifeless, until Pastor Graff got up to preach.

Pastor Graff couldn't help but bring up the subject

of the snow that was supposed to come. He said he knew people were a little disappointed, but what took place over the past few days was remarkable. Wherever he went, not a word was said about holiday hassles. He didn't hear one complaint. He heard people, excited, watching, preparing. He saw people helping each other, caring about each other. Pastor Graff said the same stresses and strains were there. The lines, the rushing around, the things to do did not go away. But everyone was looking somewhere else. They were focused on the blizzard, something different, something that would affect their lives.

Pastor Graff said the blizzard affected his life too. He had to change his sermon. He was preaching on verses from Mark 13, Jesus' words calling His disciples to watch, to be alert for His coming. Pastor Graff admitted that the blizzard prediction gave him a whole new outlook on what it meant to watch for the Lord Jesus. It wasn't just a casual watching like waiting for the UPS driver to deliver a package; it was a standing-on-guard kind of watching, a watching that really shaped the lives of God's people! Just as the blizzard prediction changed people's attitudes and actions, just as the blizzard thrill made everyone a little different, so does the forecast of Jesus' work and His coming!

"What a way to go through the holidays!" Pastor Graff exclaimed. "What a wonderful example of what it is to be a Christian who experiences the thrill of what God will do!" he went on to say. Then he pointed out that all of God's people had been *blizzard watchers:* Abraham, who followed God's call, as mentioned in Hebrews 11, "was looking forward to the city with foundations, whose architect and builder is God" (verse 10). "All these people," the writer of Hebrews went on to say, "were still living by faith when they died. They did not receive the things promised; they only saw them and welcomed them from a distance. And they admitted that they were aliens and strangers on earth. … Instead they were longing for a better country—a heavenly one!" And Moses, Pastor Graff quoted from verse 26, " 'regarded disgrace for the sake of Christ as of greater value than the treasures of Egypt, because he was looking ahead to his reward.' *Blizzard watchers!*" Pastor Graff said. "Life as a Christian is the thrill of Jesus on the cross for the forgiveness of sins and the *blizzard* of grace and mercy for us!"

Then he quoted a bunch of snow passages from the Bible. Ernest thought that was cool. "Though your sins are like scarlet, they shall be as white as snow" (Isaiah 1:18). Life under the Lord Jesus is the thrill of God's Word coming with a *blizzard* of life, of hope, of nourishment for our lives. "As the rain and the snow come down from heaven, and do not return to it without watering the earth and making it bud and flourish … so is My word that goes out from My mouth," said the Lord in Isaiah 55:10–11. "It will not return to Me empty, but will accomplish what I desire and achieve the purpose for which I sent it." Life as one of God's people is the thrill of Baptism that brings the *blizzard* of forgiveness, life, and salvation—a changed, brand-new cared-for life! "Wash me, and I will be whiter than snow," Psalm 51 declares.

"In a tiring, hard-driving, hectic, and sometimes frightening life," Pastor Graff said, "what a blessing it is, what a thrill, to watch, to look out, to live the excitement of what God will do for you!"

Things really seemed to click with all the people gathered for church that snowless Sunday morning. Ernest saw it too. This is the way it is for a Christian. It's life on the edge of a *blizzard*, a wonderful outpouring of God's work in any situation. The tone was set for a wonderful Advent for the people of St. Luke Lutheran Church. They came in a little down and disappointed. But they were leaving with a new reason to *look out!* The holiday crunch of activity wouldn't be the same. Even Pastor Graff, with all the work and preparation that this time of year brought, realized a new sense of excitement. It wasn't just another Christmas season. It was *blizzard watching!* From the manger to the cross to their little town in Michigan to his life, it was keeping watch, looking out for the great work of their Lord Jesus through it all! What was coming? What would He do with each day, with each task? *Blizzard watching!*

The day was good for the Thorpe family. That night, after Ernest said his prayers and heard everyone go to bed, he got up to look out his bedroom window. He pulled the curtain aside and saw snow falling! Flakes the size of silver dollars were blanketing the ground! At just the right time. There was no doubt: the thrill of the blizzard was not over!

STARTING RIGHT

· ·

When Christmas gets closer, there is no doubt that tension builds. It's easy to get overwhelmed by the holiday crunch and all the tasks that come with that very full time of the year. It's no different in Harrison Town.

True, Harrison Town is a small town, but it is mighty when it comes to its winter activity and preparation! Christmas was coming, and the folks in Harrison Town were getting ready. Most of the Christmas decorations were up before the big Thanksgiving weekend snow hit. But with 22 inches on the ground, and the week's delay because of snow plowing, it was a mad rush to get Main Street's light poles decked out with Christmas wreaths and lights.

With snow-covered highways, Harrison Town citizens stayed in town to do most of their Christmas shopping. The Ben Franklin five and dime had a toy sale that brought out the biggest crowd ever. The store set a sales record and also a parking lot traffic-jam record! The owners of the Jackpine Restaurant, which shared the lot with the Ben Franklin, were irritated by the sudden glut of automobiles. They complained that their customers had no place to park.

Over at the state park, employees were frantic because the sudden snow brought carloads of cross-country skiers eager to hit the trails well before the paths could be groomed or prepared!

And one of Sheriff Pankow's new deputies, Officer Hill, while doing a routine check of the Christmas display lights by the Budd Lake public access, phoned the sheriff with some bad news. He checked some tampering of the display, and now the squad car wouldn't start. The sheriff asked what was wrong. Officer Hill said he thought it was water in the carburetor. Well, Sheriff Pankow knew that Officer Hill was no mechanic. "How do you know?" the sheriff asked.

Officer Hill replied quietly, "Because the car rolled into the lake."

Yes, it was a busy time in Harrison Town. And the *busyness* was leading to some real *grumpiness!*

Pastor Graff, the dedicated servant of the Lord, also suffered from the attitude-deteriorating effects that can come with the busyness of the season. The Sunday after the blizzard he preached about John the Baptist. He was the one who did preparation. He was to make straight paths in a crooked and confused world. He was to fill in the valleys of people's emptiness. He was to smooth out the mountains, the obstacles that stood in the way of the Savior. He was to level out the rough ground, the hearts of the people, so they could be ready for Jesus.

But Pastor Graff had a hard time getting through the rough ground himself. Because of the blizzard his wife was stuck at the airport in Detroit. She couldn't make it home after her trip to visit relatives. The day before, when Pastor Graff walked into his house after making a hospital visit, he discovered that their now one-and-a-half-year-old labrador had broken through the kitchen doggie gate. The dog's first area of interest was the Christmas tree Pastor Graff had cut down on his own property and decorated to surprise his wife. It was torn up. Pastor Graff followed the path of pine needles and light strands and found the dog in his basement office finishing dessert—Pastor Graff's sermon notes for Advent and Christmas. The valleys were pretty low and the mountains pretty high, even for Pastor Graff.

As the Thorpe family left church that morning, Mr. and Mrs. Thorpe could tell that Pastor Graff was feeling low. Ernest, their already-asking-if-he-could-drive eighth-grade son, didn't pay much attention. He wanted to get home to start snooping around the house for presents. Karen, now about five and one-half years old, must have seen that Pastor Graff needed a pick-me-up. She tugged on his robe and said, "My mom and I are going to make you some special chocolate chip cookie squares!" Pastor Graff smiled, but he had lots to do. Cookies didn't seem to be the answer.

At the Thorpe home it was a busy Sunday afternoon. Finally, however, Karen convinced her mom to make the special chocolate chip cookie squares. These were no ordinary squares. What made them special was Karen's plan to decorate each one with a Christmas picture or message. She used red and green and yellow and blue decorating gel. Karen drew the pictures, and Mrs. Thorpe wrote the words. They put one dozen squares on a plate, covered them with aluminum foil, and headed over to Pastor Graff's house.

When Pastor Graff answered the door, Karen and

Mrs. Thorpe could see that he had just gotten off the ladder next to his Christmas tree. It was a mess. Pastor Graff explained what had happened, tried to chuckle a little bit, but couldn't really hide the fact that he wasn't happy about trying to salvage the tree and decorate it again. He had a lot to do, and this didn't help. Mrs. Thorpe said that she and Karen didn't want to delay him, but here were the special chocolate chip cookie squares Karen had promised. Pastor Graff was grateful. As Mrs. Thorpe and Karen turned to go, Karen said to Pastor Graff, "Look at the valleys!"

Pastor Graff closed the front door, sat down, and uncovered the plate. On every chocolate chip cookie square was a picture of a valley that was filled in—a green valley filled with red decorating gel. Around the picture were the words *Jesus Is the Reason.*

Pastor Graff looked at that plateful of cookies. The words he quoted from Isaiah 40 that morning in church came to mind: "Every valley shall be raised up, every mountain and hill made low; the rough ground shall become level, the rugged places a plain. And the glory of the LORD will be revealed."

Pastor Graff thought of John the Baptist, whose purpose was to prepare the hearts and lives of people for Jesus. John the Baptist was the one who called the people to stop, to see their valleys of emptiness and mountains of distraction, to look through the busyness and crunch of life, so they could see their need for a Savior.

Pastor Graff though about how easy it is to be consumed with emptiness and busyness and frustration at this time of year. He looked at the dozen messages staring him in the face. Filled-in valleys. "Jesus Is the Reason." The chocolate chip cookie squares were right. This time of year was not for living in the valleys, but for getting them filled in by Jesus, who came to our hectic world and gave His life on the cross to forgive, comfort, care, and fill in the valleys of emptiness apart from Him. This time of year is for real preparation—to be filled up by the life and salvation of our Lord so we can meet life that gets hectic and hard, so we can live with the hope and joy of Jesus with us now and a home in heaven. This time of year is to see the busy work of our Savior tending to our every need, filling us up, preparing us, so we can show His light and love to each other through it all!

The chocolate chip cookie squares were right—all the preparation this time of year is for a reason, a wonderful reason, a reason to celebrate! God with us in Jesus, His Son, our Savior!

Pastor Graff took a deep breath, sat back in his chair, and ate a few of those delicious squares. It might not have been John the Baptist, but a very special messenger was sent to his house that day! Not with clothing made of camel's hair or with a desert diet in hand, but with some very special chocolate chip cookie squares! He thanked the Lord for little Karen Thorpe. Then he stood up and got busy with that Christmas tree. It was Advent, and by the grace of God, he was starting right!

GETTING BETTER

If you feel like you have a grasp of Ernest Thorpe's personality by now, you could probably predict his reaction to the Christmas wrapping-paper sale that the students of Harrison Town Middle School were asked to take part in. You would probably be even more certain of your prediction if you were told that this sale was not just to give the students the satisfaction of raising money for more computer stations and science equipment, but they could win *prizes*! Prizes! Ernest Thorpe didn't want just any prize. He wanted the Huntsman axe, "the deluxe cutting instrument for every man of the woods," the prize catalog said. In order to get the Huntsman axe, Ernest had to sell $500 worth of Christmas wrapping paper.

Ernest got right to work. He gave an order form and brochure to his dad to take to the brooch factory and another set to his mom to take to choir practice and to the ladies group at church. He even gave one to his grandma to take to the American Legion Hall, where she was cashier for Sunday brunch and bingo nights. All that was left for Ernest to do was to talk to his 12 aunts and uncles and their spouses on his dad's side of the family. Along with learning the fine art of delegation, Ernest hit the $500 mark in sales with no problem. And he got the Huntsman axe, "the deluxe cutting instrument for every man of the woods."

The next question was this: What would he do with it? As he walked home on a chilly December afternoon with his new axe in its tan leather case, Ernest saw the obvious answer: Christmas tree. Why not use his new Huntsman axe to cut down a Christmas tree! Ernest let his dad know about the idea. As Ernest eyeballed a pine tree in the front yard, his father quickly suggested a Christmas tree farm. Ernest agreed and planned the outing for the next day, Saturday, December 18. He would finally use his Huntsman axe, "the deluxe cutting instrument for every man of the woods." That evening Mr. and Mrs. Thorpe had to convince Ernest that if he was going to put the axe next to his pillow while he slept, he better keep the cover on it.

All this was fine. Ernest's excitement and the plan to cut down the Christmas tree were wonderful. But one detail was overlooked. Saturday, December 18, was Mrs. Thorpe's birthday. Her husband and son left early in the morning and left no card or present. Even though Mrs. Thorpe tried not to get discouraged, she felt pretty low.

Ernest and his dad got back just after lunch with a beautiful tree. Ernest reenacted how he cut it down with his Huntsman axe, "the deluxe cutting instrument for every man of the woods." He almost chopped through the dining room table leg as he demonstrated his technique. Mrs. Thorpe was glad to see his excitement and the beautiful tree, but there was still no birthday acknowledgment. Well, she thought, maybe the best birthday present will be a great family time trimming the tree.

That thought was short-lived. First the lights didn't work. Mr. Thorpe ended up going to three stores to find new multicolored lights. The best he got was the promise to order them with a delivery date in mid-January.

Meanwhile at home, Ernest didn't want to help put ornaments up. To top it off, his axe fell on an antique ornament that Mrs. Thorpe's mother had given to her. It was beyond repair. Mrs. Thorpe's mother died a few years ago, and this ornament was very special.

Mr. Thorpe returned home with plain white lights. He mentioned that he saw Mildred Lewis at the store. She asked him to remind Mrs. Thorpe that she was to bring three dozen cookies to Karen's kindergarten Christmas program on Monday. Then Ernest and Karen started throwing tinsel at each other. That was it. Mrs. Thorpe left the room in tears. She went into her bedroom and closed the door.

As Mr. Thorpe stood in the living room looking at his tinsel-covered children and holding a tangled mess of three hundred white lights, he remembered. It was December 18! He had *never* forgotten his wife's birthday. Mr. Thorpe told Ernest to put the Huntsman axe away. Then he knocked on the bedroom door and told his wife they'd be back in a little while. Mr. Thorpe loaded the kids into the truck and went over to Tagliamonte's Restaurant to get some of his wife's favorite mostaccioli for supper. Then he stopped at the IGA for some roses and neapolitan ice cream—another favorite of Mrs. Thorpe.

When they got home, Mrs. Thorpe was sitting quietly in the living room reading her Bible. They greeted her with repentant looks and hearts and birthday hugs and kisses. They served Mom her favorite dishes, put the roses in a vase, and placed a candle in a slab of neapolitan ice cream. After a chorus of "Happy Birthday to You" and "We're sorry we forgot," Ernest and Karen were sent off to get ready for bed. Things were getting better.

Mr. Thorpe cleaned up the supper dishes and sat on the couch next to Mrs. Thorpe. They looked at the partially lighted Christmas tree. Mr. Thorpe turned to his wife of 16 years and said, "I'm sorry." Mrs. Thorpe said it wasn't just her birthday that was giving her the blues. And it wasn't just the kids. She missed her mom. She felt overwhelmed.

"It was everything, I guess," she said. "But I read something while you were gone." Mrs. Thorpe opened her Bible to Isaiah 61. She read this for her husband:

> The Spirit of the Sovereign LORD is on Me, because the LORD has anointed Me to preach good news to the poor. He has sent Me to bind up the brokenhearted, to proclaim freedom for the captives and release from darkness for the prisoners, to proclaim the year of the LORD's favor and the day of vengeance of our God, to comfort all who mourn, and provide for those who grieve in Zion—to bestow on them a crown of beauty instead of ashes, the oil of gladness instead of mourning, and a garment of praise instead of a spirit of despair.

Mrs. Thorpe said to her husband, "Sometimes I forget that my blues are what Christmas—what Jesus—is for." Mr. Thorpe smiled, put his arm around his wife, and they sat quietly listening to Christmas music and looking at the tree.

Ernest was, of course, out of bed and had his ear next to his slightly opened door, listening to his parents talk. It was another helping of the right thing to hear.

It was another Christmas that the Thorpes needed—another Christmas to learn why Jesus came. From the manger to the cross, through the water of Baptism to the Word, to His body and blood in the Lord's Supper, Jesus was present with *good news*. Life and hope to *bind up broken hearts*. Forgiveness of sins to bring *freedom* from hurt and wrong. The light of truth in the middle of *dark days*. Real comfort through all grief. The gladness of God with us, for us, forever. For a mom and a family going through some tough holiday times, and for you too. The whole thing is for *getting better.*

RESOUNDING JOY!

Some of you might wonder if the Thorpe family is real. Well, they're probably as real as you and your family are sometimes. One thing was very real late December in Harrison Town. School was out! The bell rang on the Friday before Christmas and that was it! Ernest delighted in the fact that there would be no more school until next year. He was free! No homework, no teachers, no bagged lunches for two weeks. No desks, no sitting still in class, no algebra story problems. Finally, complete relaxation had arrived! At least that was the general idea until Ernest walked into the kitchen that afternoon.

"Remember, you've got practice tomorrow morning bright and early!" Mrs. Thorpe said to Ernest and his sister.

Practice? She was right. It was for the Sunday school Christmas Eve service at St. Luke Lutheran Church. That meant practice, lines, memorizing. "I thought this was Christmas *vacation*," Ernest mumbled in Karen's direction.

Bright and early on Saturday morning Mr. Thorpe drove Ernest and Karen to church for practice. Ernest rode the whole way with his head pressed against the cold window of the truck door. He slunk into church. Mr. Thorpe went in with them to watch the practice.

Karen and her kindergarten class did great. They were thrilled with the Christmas service. Karen was an angel. She got to sing "Away in a Manger." Ernest was a narrator. He had two parts. One was read, the other was memorized. He had known about these parts for two weeks, but he hadn't given them any attention until that Saturday morning, and it showed. His presentation was in a monotone voice that sounded like he was talking about his next dentist appointment:

In the sixth month, God sent the angel Gabriel to Nazareth, a town in Galilee, to a virgin pledged to be married to a man named Joseph, a descendant of David. The virgin's name was Mary. The angel went to her and said, "Greetings, you who are highly favored! The Lord is with you."

Mary was greatly troubled at his words and wondered what kind of greeting this might be. But the angel said to her, "Do not be afraid, Mary, you have found favor with God. You will be with child and give birth to a son, and you are to give Him the name Jesus. He will be great and will be called the Son of the Most High. The Lord God will give Him the throne of His father David, and He will reign over the house of Jacob forever; His kingdom will never end."

That was the one that was read. Then he recited his memorized one, while he looked straight at his notes!

But the angel said to them, "Do not be afraid. I bring you good news of great joy that will be for all the people. Today in the town of David a Savior has been born to you; He is Christ the Lord."

Ernest was not ready. Inside his tired mind he

thought, I've heard all this before. I'm in eighth grade. I want to relax. I want to have fun. This makes me sick.

It was at that moment, when the word *sick* came into his mind, that Ernest's Christmas Eve Service Evasion Scheme was born. I'll be sick, he thought. And when Mrs. Schliefmann, the Sunday school superintendent, announced that there would be more practice after church tomorrow, Ernest could almost feel a queasy stomach coming on.

Sunday morning arrived. When Mrs. Thorpe went to get Ernest up for church, he rolled over in his bed and let out a dramatic, "Ooohh, I don't feel good at all."

Upon inquiry from Mom, Ernest revealed that his stomach really hurt. She was just about to tuck him in and get him some crackers and 7-Up when he added some fateful words: "It doesn't look like I'll be able to go to church or to practice."

His cover was blown. Mrs. Thorpe replied, "Well, this must be pretty serious, Ernest. I'm going to check with your dad about calling the doctor."

Ernest started sweating. His father came in and felt his forehead. "It might be appendicitis," Mr. Thorpe said. As he walked out of the bedroom he added, "I'm going to call the doctor to see if he is available for surgery on Sunday mornings."

Ernest suddenly appeared in the kitchen looking remarkably well. "Maybe a little 7-Up will help," he said bravely. "I think I'll make it."

Ernest did make it in body, but not in mind. Mrs. Schliefmann wondered if they would ever be ready for Christmas Eve.

Ernest finally managed to memorize his lines by the

time Christmas Eve morning came. For supper the family would head to Clare for a buffet supper at Ponderosa. It was a family tradition. They used to go to the Swedish Manor Smorgasbord, but that closed a few years ago. As the Thorpe family drove to Clare, snow began to fall. They went into Ponderosa and sat by a window. When Ernest looked at the streetlight he could see the big snowflakes filling the air. The old, half-melted, dirt-covered snow from the Thanksgiving blizzard was covered up by the brand new. Christmas music was playing as the Thorpe family ate their supper. Ernest wore a tie, Karen a pretty Christmas dress.

When everyone was just about finished eating, Mrs. Thorpe said, "Ernest, Karen, your father and I have some important news for you." The Thorpe children listened. And their mother continued. "I'm going to have a baby. You're going to have a new brother or sister."

A baby! Wow! What a great surprise! What great news! Right away Ernest asked about names and about how he could help with his baby brother. Karen asked about how she could help and play with her new baby sister. Mr. and Mrs. Thorpe were thrilled to see their children's excitement and joy.

On the way to the Christmas Eve service, Ernest thought about his lines. The angel's words to Mary: "You will be with child and give birth to a son, and you are to give Him the name Jesus. He will be great and will be called the Son of the Most High."

And the angel's words to the shepherds: "I bring you good news of great joy that will be for all the people. Today in the town of David a Savior has been born to you; He is Christ the Lord."

Mary must have felt just like he did, Ernest

thought. The shepherds too. Excitement, a new life, wonder about the future, joy—lots of joy! And that baby was Jesus, the Savior. If a baby in his own family caused so much joyful expectation, Ernest thought, what great joy must have happened when the baby was Jesus! What great joy to know that the answer to what people had prayed for was coming! New life and help, forgiveness and the presence of God, all in Jesus—wow! As Mr. Thorpe drove carefully through the snow back to Harrison Town, Ernest realized that Christmas was much more than an interruption in his school vacation. It was a time of joy, the joy of what is brand new, the joy of the gift of life, the joy of something more than the routine. It was Jesus, every day, doing His work from the manger to the cross to now. And what great work He did—a new baby in the Thorpe family included!

The Christmas Eve service began on time and with a full church. Ernest could see his mom and dad smiling as he stood up front. He said his parts as though he meant them. And he did.

After the Christmas service, Ernest heard people saying to Mrs. Schliefmann, "Well, it's all over. Now you can relax. You did a good job." But as Ernest went home and went to sleep, he knew that, really, this was just the beginning! While in previous years the thought of presents kept him awake on Christmas Eve, this year it was the thought of a baby. When it's for you it means a lot. This year Ernest's eyes were wide open as he prayed a prayer of thanks. This year he saw God's work, and with it resounding joy!

V

STORIES OF LIFE

A FALSE ALARM

Summers in Harrison Town are nothing but inviting! Budd Lake beckons swimmers, boaters, and fishermen. The warm August breezes spread the wealth of smells that come from the county fair—fresh-baked elephant ears, egg rolls in the Chinese food trailer, and a great gathering of cows, horses, and more in the livestock barns (well, that smell might not exactly be inviting). The people are inviting too, welcoming the mix of visitors and longtime residents.

New visitors are always welcome in Harrison Town. One young man—a six-foot-four high school football player—moved to Harrison Town with his family during the summer. The football coach was glad to welcome him! He had to check and see, however, whether this new addition to the squad would be cut because of the academic requirements of the district. First, the coach asked the new player, "How tall are you?"

The player placed his hand on his forehead and proceeded to measure handbreadth by handbreadth all the way down to his toes. "Six feet, four inches, sir," he answered. Next the coach asked him how old he was.

The young man began to count his fingers, then proceeded to his toes. Finally he answered, "Sixteen, sir."

The last question the coach asked was, "What's your name, son?"

The young man began to nod his head in a rhythmic motion: *nod nod-nod-nod nod-nod. Nod nod-nod-nod nod-nod. Nod nod-nod-nod-nod.* Then he stopped and replied, "Dennis, sir."

The coach was puzzled. "Son, I understand how you got your height. I understand how you got your age. But what were you doing when I asked your name?"

The player answered in song: "Happy birthday to you. Happy birthday to you. Happy birthday dear Dennis!"

Yes, new visitors are welcome and provide plenty of excitement. You might remember that the Thorpes were waiting for a new visitor. A baby was due! Their parents revealed the good news to Ernest and Karen last Christmas Eve. What a thrill! It was more of a thrill than Ernest and his sister realized. Mr. and Mrs. Thorpe had almost given up hope. They had been trying to have another child for about five years. And when they least expected it, they received a great answer to their prayers! The baby was on its way! Since Mrs. Thorpe was in her late 30s, however, the pregnancy was considered high risk.

And high risk it was, especially for Mr. Thorpe. This baby thing was not as simple as it used to be. There were so many new tests to undergo, more forms to fill out. He even had to go to a class so he and his wife could learn to breathe! Mr. Thorpe thought he had mastered that already. Everything seemed a little backwards. The first baby picture was taken before the baby was born instead of after. Karen, the Thorpes' six-year-old daughter, wanted to put the ultrasound picture of her *sister* on the fridge. Ernest said that he'd be glad to have his little *brother's* photo displayed. Then there were the baby items. The room was ready at home. It even had a battery-operated baby swing. Mr. Thorpe thought that was high risk! It looked like it could take off! Even diaper sizes were moving beyond his understanding. There was no more *small, medium* and *large.* Now he had to find where the baby might fit within a range of terms that seemed to go from "not moving very much" to "pole vaulter." Then there was good old Doc Martin. Doc Martin had delivered Ernest and Karen. But with all the new procedures, and with the high-risk pregnancy, Doc Martin was out of the picture. A new young doctor from the Clare hospital took charge. Nothing was simple anymore. Mr. Thorpe was thrown for a loop!

Ernest never saw his dad this jumpy before. He was usually cool, calm, and collected. But not anymore! The due date for the baby was August 13. As that day approached, Mr. Thorpe showed more and more signs of nervousness. He paced around and forgot what he came into rooms for. He jumped when the phone rang. Mrs. Thorpe was not very happy with her husband's behavior. After all, who was carrying the baby? She kept saying to her husband, "Relax!"

Then it happened. It was a sunny August afternoon, just a few days before the due date. Mrs. Thorpe was sitting on a blanket at the edge of the garden getting some sun and doing some weeding. She felt something. Could it be? Contractions? After about 15 minutes, she got up, went into the house, and interrupted Ernest's mid-afternoon Nintendo game. "Ernest," she said as calmly as possible, "I'm going to call your father at work. Would you please get the bag I packed and put it by the door?"

Ernest's eyes opened wide. It was not very often that he was speechless or that he left a video game at mid-play. But he got up to get that bag in no time. Then Mrs. Thorpe spoke calmly to her husband on the phone. "I think it's time," she said. "Would you come and drive me to the hospital?"

At the brooch factory, Mr. Thorpe answered calmly. He told his wife that he would come right home. She should sit down and do her breathing until he arrived. Mrs. Thorpe was surprised at how in control he sounded! Perhaps he had regrouped and was back to his old self! After 15 minutes of breathing exercises and waiting, the phone rang. Mrs. Thorpe answered. It was her dear hubby. Mr. Thorpe explained that he got in his truck, put it into gear to pull away, but discovered it was in the wrong gear. In his excitement he put it into *R* instead of *D*. His truck bolted backwards, hit a dumpster, and jumped two curbs. His truck—now attached by the bumper to the dumpster—was blocking the driveway at the brooch factory. They were picking up the garbage, but a tow truck was needed to free his truck. Mr. Thorpe wondered if a neighbor could drive his wife to Clare. He promised to meet her there as soon as possible.

Mrs. Thorpe knew it was too good to be true. She really thought her husband should relax. What else could go wrong? After calling several neighbors, she found out. No one was around! She even tried to get in touch with Pastor Graff. He wasn't in either. Finally Mrs. Thorpe said to Ernest, "Ernest, hold down the fort. I'm going to drive myself to Clare. I'll call you when I get there." The contractions weren't too strong, so Mrs. Thorpe knew she'd be able to make it.

Mrs. Thorpe arrived safely at the Clare hospital. A half hour later, Mr. Thorpe rushed into the emergency room. Mrs. Thorpe had one word to say to her husband, "Relax." It turned out to be a false alarm. Apparently Mrs. Thorpe had been exerting herself a bit too much pulling those weeds. The doctor told her to take it easy. It probably wouldn't be too long now. After many apologies and a promise that she wouldn't have to cook that evening, Mr. Thorpe escorted his wife out of the emergency room and they headed home.

They stopped at the Remedy Restaurant for some tacos to take home for supper. Ernest and Karen were glad to see their parents back at home, even though there was no baby yet. The Thorpe family gathered around the supper table. Mr. Thorpe led the devotion about Jesus, the bread of life. Mr. Thorpe read Jesus' words:

I am the living bread that came down from heaven. If anyone eats of this bread, he will live forever. This bread is My flesh, which I will give for the life of the world.

The bread of life. For the life of the world. Mr. Thorpe realized that he had been worried about life—his baby's life in this high-risk pregnancy, his wife's life through a time that wasn't easy, his own life as he was about to become a father again. Would the baby be okay? Would his wife come through the delivery all right?

Would he be a good father for his new child? Would he be able to support his growing family? Would he be able to give the time needed to love all of his children? In answer to these *alarming* things, here was the bread of life. Jesus for the *life* of the world. Here was his Savior, who was taking good care of that little baby still waiting to be born. Here was Jesus surrounding Mrs. Thorpe with care and protection. And here was Jesus, who gave His life for a new dad too. Jesus was the bread of life for *false alarms.* He showed that clearly! Jesus was the bread of life for *real alarms* too—everything that was so *alarming* through each day.

Mr. Thorpe prayed the prayer of blessing before everyone dug into the tacos. He thanked the bread of life for providing the food the family was about to enjoy. And he thanked the bread of life for the very real *new life* that He gave. As the Thorpe children began devouring tacos, Mr. Thorpe placed his hand on his wife's, looked into her eyes, and said, "I think I'll just relax." Mrs. Thorpe smiled and squeezed his hand.

And the wait went on. The exciting wait to welcome the newest visitor to Harrison Town, Michigan, would last a little longer! But there was no doubt, in the middle of the *alarming, new life* had already arrived!

TO WHOM SHALL WE GO?

The tension-filled expectation of waiting for a baby to be born got to be too much for Ernest. Sure, things settled down a little bit after the false alarm, but Ernest was used to peaceful summers—at least peaceful in his own way. Ernest had his fill of being ready every day, staying close to home, and curtailing normal summer fun. Finally, however, he saw a glimmer of hope in the middle of baby-crunch time. The opportunity arose for him to have a bit of late-summer relief. Paul Tucker invited Ernest to attend the annual Tucker family picnic and fishing outing. Paul's family was glad to take Ernest along. There would be food, games, and great fishing! The picnic took place near a lake about two hours northwest of Harrison Town. Ernest would have to be ready to leave at seven o'clock Saturday morning. That was no problem! Getting up early on Saturday was a small price to pay for a little relief!

At least relief is what Ernest thought he would get. The Tuckers swung by Ernest's house at about 7:20.

Ernest loaded his fishing gear into the Tuckers' station wagon and climbed in. He was ready to roll! Mrs. Tucker apologized to Ernest for being late. She said Mr. Tucker didn't have the energy to get ready in time. He wasn't very enthusiastic when it came to spending time with his family, Ernest was informed. Now it was 7:30. They hadn't even pulled out of the driveway. Ernest saw Paul and his sister rolling their eyes. Paul whispered to Ernest, "I hope you enjoy the trip."

This *was* a new experience for Ernest. As they pulled out of the driveway Mr. Tucker adjusted the radio to his favorite station so he could hear Paul Harvey. "I love Paul Harvey," Mr. Tucker commented. He started doing Paul Harvey imitations: "Good day! Page two!" While Mr. Tucker was in the middle of imitating a Bunn coffee maker commercial, Mrs. Tucker changed the radio station to the music station she enjoyed. Mr. Tucker changed it back. "I want to hear Paul Harvey," he said.

Mrs. Tucker turned the radio volume down. "I have a headache," she said, then leaned her head back on the headrest and closed her eyes. Mr. Tucker proceeded to lean close to the speaker to hear Paul Harvey. His head was almost against the car door as he drove. Mrs. Tucker opened her eyes and shouted, "What are you doing? Watch where you're going! We've got children in the car!"

Mr. Tucker sat up straight, looked at his wife, and turned the radio up. "I just want to hear Paul Harvey," he said firmly. Ernest looked at his friend Paul. Paul just looked out the window. As a matter-of-fact, Paul's sister and mom were looking out their windows too. It was silent in the car now, except for the voice of Paul Harvey saying, "Good day!"

Ernest was sitting in the middle of the backseat, so he really didn't have anything to lean on. All he could do was sit up straight and look out the windshield of the car. Everyone in the car was sleeping now, except for him and Mr. Tucker. But Ernest thought he saw Mr. Tucker's eyes getting heavy. Ernest tried to cough. Loudly. Maybe that would keep Mr. Tucker awake. Mr. Tucker was going pretty fast. Ernest thought about how nice it would be to hang around the house with his mom. That's when they hit the bump! Ernest could never figure out exactly where the bump was after those BUMP signs on the highway. But there was no doubt about this one. Ernest thought he saw Mrs. Tucker's head hit the roof of the car. Judging by her reaction, it must have hurt! "What was that?" Mrs. Tucker exclaimed. "Are you falling asleep?"

"No, I'm not falling asleep. I never fall asleep!" Mr. Tucker replied. "We hit a bump. I'm not the highway commissioner. I can't control the bumps."

Mrs. Tucker looked at the gas gauge. "You better stop for gas," she said. "I'm sure these kids need to get out and stretch anyway. Does anyone need to go to the bathroom?" Mrs. Tucker turned around and looked into the back seat for a reply. No one said anything.

Ernest said quietly, "I'm fine, thank you." Mrs. Tucker persisted. "You better stop," she told her husband.

"We've got plenty of gas," he piped back. "You're just looking at the wrong angle. We'll fill up when we get there. It's cheaper." Ernest looked at the gas gauge. He wondered how far a car could travel when the gas gauge was reading *E*. Ernest was glad he wore his hiking boots.

Finally Mr. Tucker took an exit off the highway. He drove to the stop sign at the bottom of the ramp and turned right. Mrs. Tucker spoke up, "What are you doing? Where are you going?"

"To the lake!" Mr. Tucker answered.

"You're supposed to turn *left*," Mrs. Tucker directed.

"I know where I'm going," Mr. Tucker replied.

Mrs. Tucker opened the glove compartment and started searching for the map. "I know where I'm going!" Mr. Tucker said more firmly. After about 20 minutes, Mr. Tucker pulled into a parking lot and turned around.

"Why don't you just stop and ask somebody?" Mrs. Tucker asked. Mr. Tucker was silent. "We're going to be late," Mrs. Tucker went on to say. Mr. Tucker came to the highway and proceeded in the correct direction. "I won't say I told you so," Mrs. Tucker started to say.

"Then don't!" Mr. Tucker shouted back. Ernest saw Paul's eyes open and roll. He sighed and looked at Ernest.

"You better be in a good mood for your mother," Mrs. Tucker told her husband.

Mr. Tucker replied with a question: "Did you bring the beans?"

Mrs. Tucker cringed. "The beans," she repeated with regret in her voice.

Mr. Tucker went on, "You mean you forgot the beans! What's a Tucker family picnic without the beans? You know my mother can't make the beans anymore! We're really gonna hear about this! All we have to do is

126

bring the beans, and you forget the beans." Mr. Tucker's voice trailed off in disgust.

What a ride this had been! When Mr. Tucker turned into a beautiful wooded area, Ernest sighed with relief. He could see a lake glistening in the sunlight. The car stopped and everybody tumbled out. Ernest felt like he was released from a time capsule—back into the real world with fresh air and the wonderful sounds of creation around him. Ernest and Paul hit the ground running. It was a perfect summer day! Paul's dad put the boat in the lake while Paul's mom and sister mixed with the family and set up a picnic table. Fishing was the first order of business at these outings, Paul told Ernest. If they could catch some fish for lunch, the day would be a real success.

Mr. Tucker rounded up the boys and said to his wife and daughter, "Okay, ladies, let's go fishing! Mom, I need you to drive the boat while the fishermen go after their prey!" Mrs. Tucker did not like the fact that she always had to drive the boat. According to her husband she never did it right anyway. This time she opted out of boat driving to stay on land and talk with Mr. Tucker's sister. Mr. Tucker was not happy with the decision.

Ernest took a chance and said, "I'll be glad to drive the boat, Mr. Tucker."

"Fine, Ernest," he answered. Off they went.

Ernest loved fishing. His dad taught him a lot about it. His dad taught him about fish and fishing safety. There wasn't much conversation on the boat, but after a couple of hours they were at their limit. Ernest was thrilled with the result and was ready for lunch! They docked the boat, brought their catch on shore, and cleaned the fish. Everyone dug in pretty quickly, but Ernest paused silently to say a prayer of thanks—just like at home. It was a delicious lunch—perch and bass cooked over an open fire. Even without the beans the meal was great!

Mr. Tucker decided to take a nap after lunch. Paul's sister played with her cousins, Mrs. Tucker talked with relatives. Paul and Ernest decided to take a hike in the woods. As they walked they talked about the fish they caught and the ones that got away. They talked about the Detroit Tigers and about how summertime was the best. Then Ernest asked Paul about the car ride: "Do your parents like each other?"

"They're married, aren't they?" Paul replied.

Paul stopped and sat down on a big rock. Ernest sat down too. It was great to be in the woods. It was so quiet. Paul and Ernest sat and listened to nothing. Ernest could see that Paul was sad, and then he realized that Paul looked like that every day. They sat there until it was time to head home. It looked like Paul wished he could freeze the peaceful moment. He didn't want to leave. Ernest finally said, "I'll race you to the car!" The boys took off running.

The car ride home was very quiet. But it wasn't a quiet like in the woods. This quiet seemed quite loud and tense. The Tuckers dropped Ernest off at home at about five o'clock—suppertime. Ernest thanked the Tuckers for the wonderful fishing time and waved to Paul as the family drove off. When Ernest walked inside his house he was greeted by his mom and dad and sister. Ernest's dad was wearing an apron. "Ernest," his dad said, "you're just in time! Mom was in the mood for some mostaccioli and kiwi. The fruit is on the table, and the pasta is ready. Why don't you wash up and join us. I want to hear how many fish you caught!"

Ernest smiled and made his way toward the bathroom. He could hear his mom and sister laughing about kiwi and his dad's apron as he went down the hallway. As Ernest turned to go into the bathroom, the wall in the hallway caught his eye. It was his parents' wedding wall. Hanging on the wall were some wedding pictures, a framed wedding bulletin, and some wedding mementos with sayings on them that his parents had received. Ernest never paid much attention to the wall, but something caught his eye this time. There were two framed pictures that had cross-stitched words. One had the title "Our Wedding Verse." It read: *Lord, to whom shall we go? You have the words of eternal life. John 6:68.* Ernest thought about everyone in the Tucker family looking out the car windows in different directions. "To whom shall we go?" Ernest read aloud. The other framed picture had the title "Our Way in Marriage." It read: *Submit to one another out of reverence for Christ.*

Wives, submit to your husbands as to the Lord. For the husband is the head of the wife as Christ is the head of the church, His body, of which He is the Savior. Now as the church voluntarily submits to Christ, so also wives should submit to their husbands in everything.

Husbands, love your wives, just as Christ loved the church and gave Himself up for her to make her holy, cleansing her by the washing with water through the word, and to present her to Himself as a radiant church, without stain or wrinkle or any other blemish, but holy and blameless. In this same way, husbands ought to love their wives as their own bodies. He who loves his wife loves himself. Ephesians 5:21–28.

Ernest thought about the outing. He thought about marriage and what giving in to each other and loving each other can do. He thought about his parents being together—with Jesus and with each other. Ernest was glad his parents lived that wedding wall. He knew how blessed the new baby would be. After washing his hands, Ernest filled in his family on his great fishing catch. He laughed along with them about the kiwi and Dad's flowered apron. Before they ate, Mr. Thorpe led the family in a prayer of thanks for the food. He included a special prayer of thanks for bringing Ernest home safely, and he asked the Lord to watch over their new little baby—whenever the time for being born might be.

Ernest was glad to be home and glad that he and his family knew to whom to go. Always.

ON THE ALERT

Still no baby. "How long does this thing take, any-way?" Ernest wondered aloud as he sat outside on a hot and humid August day. Mrs. Thorpe had wondered the same thing. It was now three days past the due date. It was not easy for Mrs. Thorpe to get around. It's got to happen sometime, Ernest thought. I wonder why we're still waiting. Mrs. Thorpe came out of the house and sat down on a lawn chair next to Ernest. The air condition-er stopped running three days ago, and a serviceman couldn't come for two more days.

"What do you think the record is for the longest pregnancy, Mom?" Ernest asked.

Mrs. Thorpe responded, "I'm not planning on set-ting any records, Ernest."

Ernest went on, "Did you know a whale can be pregnant for 16 months, but a raccoon is only pregnant for 2 months?"

Mrs. Thorpe was glad that Ernest remembered his sci-ence lessons, but she responded, "More power to the rac-coons, Ernest." Rain started to fall. Mrs. Thorpe headed down to the IGA for a few groceries and Ernest went inside.

Summer was getting long for everyone, but still it was filled with good times and plenty of excitement. Ernest and his friends enjoyed the waters of Budd Lake almost every day. Swimming races and games of "submarine" kept them cool and occupied. Fishing challenges off the "power dock" kept the boys coming back to try to catch that big muskie they knew had to be there. Of course, the annual Clare County Fair came just in time—the beginning of August—to provide a new round of thrills and adventure for Ernest and his friends.

The food at the fair was great. The bingo tent buzzed with eager adults, and the big-name concerts always sold out. But this year, the arcade was the main excitement for Ernest. He couldn't believe that such great prizes were given for winning such simple games! After Ernest surveyed the prizes on his first day at the fair, he decided on the one he wanted: a Detroit Tigers team poster. It had all the players' autographs. All you had to do was shoot a red star out of the middle of a piece of paper with a BB gun. No problem! Ernest thought. He knew how to shoot a BB gun. He could see that little red star disappearing as he shot imaginary BBs. "It's all mine," he told Andy Oreby. "That Detroit poster is all mine!"

Ernest had five dollars to spend. Each turn cost 50¢. He brought Andy over to the BB game and told him, "Watch this." Ernest lined up the sights and let the BBs fly! He grinned at Andy with expectant victory.

Then came the verdict. The man who ran the game pulled in the card, showed Ernest that he barely made a dent in that red star, and said with a smile, "Try again, son!"

Ernest couldn't believe it! He would try again! "Maybe that was a bad BB gun," he told Andy. Ernest switched guns and fired away.

The man showed him the card. "Try again, son," the man said with that smile of his. After Ernest's 10th try and the depletion of his funds, the man said, "Sorry, son, here's a spider ring for all your good effort. Keep practicing now!"

A spider ring. A plastic, flimsy spider ring! Andy tried to console Ernest, "Heh, heh, good shooting, Ernest. If you let me look at your spider ring, I'll buy you a piece of fudge!" Ernest didn't think Andy was funny at all, but he walked with him to the building where fudge was made every day.

The fudge maker stood inside a screened-in cubicle. People watched him make fudge on his marble table. His wife stood at the cash register and sold the candy. Andy ordered a slice of good old chocolate. Ernest wanted some of the chocolate-mint fudge that was being made. As he was about to place his order, Andy said, "Wait a minute! I want to see that valuable ring!" Andy's laughter was getting out of hand.

Ernest was angry and embarrassed and said, "Here, take a close look!" He wound up and threw the ring at Andy. At that moment Andy was reaching to get his piece of chocolate fudge. The fudge maker's wife was getting Andy's change. The fudge maker had turned around to clean his tools. The spider ring bounced off Andy's arm, ricocheted into the air, landed on top of the fudge maker's cubicle, fell through a hole in the screen, and sank into the very soft chocolate-mint fudge on the marble table. Ernest and Andy left feeling that their fair adventures were pretty well complete. Time to stay close to home!

The week following the fair was not quite as dramatic, but it still was exciting. You see, it was registration at high school for freshmen. Ernest was going to high school! The gym had tables everywhere. Freshmen and their parents made the rounds to choose classes, pick up orientation materials, get locks for lockers, buy gym clothes, and survey the multitude of clubs and organizations.

Ernest checked out the sports opportunities. He talked to the people at the Science Club table. Ernest liked science. He greeted the 4-H people but didn't feel inclined to get involved in any more pig-raising or the like.

Then Ernest stopped at the FCA table—the Fellowship of Christian Athletes. They had a great brochure in the shape of the school mascot—a Harrison Town Hornet. The cover said, "Be strong in the Lord and in His mighty power." Inside the brochure the verse was continued and made connections to high school sports and activities:

> Put on the full armor of God so that you can take your stand against the devil's schemes. For our struggle is not against flesh and blood, but against the rulers, against the authorities, against the powers of this dark world and against the spiritual forces of evil in the heavenly realms. Therefore put on the full armor of God, so that when the day of evil comes, you may be able to stand your ground, and after you have done everything, to stand. Stand firm then, with the belt of truth buckled around your waist, with the breastplate of

righteousness in place, and with your feet fitted with the readiness that comes from the gospel of peace. In addition to all this, take up the shield of faith, with which you can extinguish all the flaming arrows of the evil one. Take the helmet of salvation and the sword of the Spirit, which is the word of God.

It *was* a great brochure! One of the students behind the table saw Ernest's name tag and said, "Hey, Ernest, there will be a lot of challenges in high school. Our group has a great time, and we help you stay on the alert! If you're interested, let me know. My name is Michael." Ernest said thanks. He finished his registration and made sure that the Hornet brochure of the Fellowship of Christian Athletes stayed on top of his pile of papers.

That was last week. Now it was raining, and all Ernest had to do was wait. At least he thought so until the phone rang. It was Andy Oreby. "Hey, Ernest," Andy said on the other end of the phone, "I just picked up the new *Devastator* video. It's *Devastator Part V*, where the aliens come back and take over the bodies of his family. How about I bring it over and we watch it together? It's gonna be great!" Ernest agreed. It was raining—a perfect video day!

Andy arrived and popped the video into the VCR. Ernest was ready with cheese popcorn and potato chips. Ernest's first thoughts as he watched *Devastator Part V* were "Wow, this is cool!" Aliens were taking over bodies. Devastator was taking apart aliens. It was complete adventure—battle at its best. It was destruction—the cool stuff everybody liked. But as Ernest looked away from the screen for a moment to turn and get a handful of cheese popcorn, he caught a glimpse of something else. He saw the bag his mom had packed for her trip to the hospital. Next to it was a diaper bag with little lambs on it. Then he saw the pile of his high school registration material on the end table. On top of the pile was that FCA brochure that read, "Be strong in the Lord and in His mighty power." Ernest stuffed a handful of cheese popcorn into his mouth and turned back to look at the television screen. He saw aliens taking over another one of the Devastator's family members. He looked at that diaper bag again, and then at the brochure. "Andy," Ernest said, "we've got to turn this movie off."

Andy looked completely surprised. Ernest got up, pressed the stop button, and turned off the TV. "Andy, there is no way this kind of stuff can be in our house when a little baby is going to be here. It's just no good. I don't want him seeing that! What do you think it's going to do to his life? My mom and dad never had this junk in our house when I was little. Looks like it's time for me to be more alert! Let's sit on the porch."

Ernest picked up the munchies, and he and Andy sat on the porch. It was sprinkling now. Ernest and Andy talked about high school and how great the summer was. Mrs. Thorpe came home from the IGA. Andy and Ernest helped her bring in the groceries. Mrs. Thorpe said, "Ernest I found some of your favorite fudge from the fair on closeout at the IGA—chocolate mint!" Mrs. Thorpe unwrapped the slab of fudge and started to cut a slice. "What's this?" she asked as she got halfway through the first cut. "What *is* this?" She held the object up in front of Ernest and Andy.

"It looks like a spider ring, Mom," Ernest replied. "Don't worry about it. I'm sure the fudge is fine."

They each had a piece. As the waiting process continued in the Thorpe home, there was more readiness than ever before—for a baby, for watching out for spider rings, and for living their lives under the gracious life Jesus gave. They were *on the alert!*

A GIFT
FROM ABOVE

N ights in Harrison Town are wonderful. When the sky is clear, the stars command your attention. Satellites make regular trips across the celestial landscape. It's fun to spot them and follow their paths. And it's so quiet. No big-city noises intrude into the peaceful small-town setting. Sure, there's the occasional car with no muffler hot-rodding down Main Street, but quiet is the prevailing sound of nighttime in Harrison Town.

One exception, of course, is a summer thunderstorm! What a thunderstorm it was that humid August evening while the Thorpes were still waiting for their baby to be born. At dusk the sky clouded up, and the wind and rain began an hour or so later. Then came the thunder and lightning. Ernest and Karen were already in bed when the crashes of thunder began. The rain beat against the house and the lightning seemed nonstop. This was a big storm. After midnight the electricity went out. Mr. Thorpe lay awake in bed, just listening. Mrs. Thorpe was doing the same. Ernest and Karen were not sleeping either.

But the noise of the storm was not the most significant noise that night in the Thorpe home. As Mr. and Mrs. Thorpe lay in bed in the wee hours of the morning, in the middle of lightning, thunder, wind, and rain, Mrs. Thorpe spoke two words that commanded Mr. Thorpe's attention.

"It's time."

It's time! Mr. Thorpe sat up in bed. "You mean, it's *time?*" he asked, pointing to Mrs. Thorpe's stomach.

Mrs. Thorpe answered, "Yes. I think we better go right now."

"Right now?" Mr. Thorpe echoed. Mrs. Thorpe shook her head yes. Thunder crashed. Mr. Thorpe gulped and got out of bed. He put some clothes on and said to his wife, "You get ready, I'll get the truck." Mr. Thorpe dashed out the bedroom door and then outside into the rain.

Ernest and Karen appeared in the bedroom doorway. "What's going on, Mom?" Ernest asked.

"It's time to head to the hospital," Mrs. Thorpe answered.

Things were happening fast. Mr. Thorpe came back into the house. He was soaked. "The truck battery is dead," he said. "I put the keys in it last night just in case. The door was ajar and the dome light drained the battery."

"Can't we use the car?" Mrs. Thorpe asked.

"The garage-door opener doesn't work with the power out, and I can't get into the garage," Mr. Thorpe answered.

"Where are the keys?" his wife countered.

"I put them in the car. I wanted to be ready." Thunder crashed again. "I'll call someone," Mr. Thorpe went on. He picked up the phone. No dial tone. Thunder crashed. Mrs. Thorpe was getting uncomfortable. Mr. Thorpe had his wife lie down. He turned to Ernest. "Ernest, I've got a job for you. I have to stay here with Mom. I want you to get dressed and ride down to Doc Martin's place. Wake him up and tell him that we need him. Mom's gonna have this baby real soon. Do you understand?"

"Sure, Dad," Ernest replied. His heart was pounding. This was important. Thunder crashed again.

His dad said, "Stay low and be careful." Mr. Thorpe then asked Karen to watch out the front window for Doc Martin's car and to call out when she saw it.

Ernest ran out into the rain and grabbed his bike from its spot underneath the porch. He hopped on it and made his way down the hill toward Doc Martin's. Lightning lit up the sky and thunder crashed. The force of the rain made Ernest squint as he watched the road. Ernest prayed, "Dear Jesus, get me to Doc Martin's safely and take care of Mom."

Doc Martin's house wasn't far away. When Ernest got off the muddy, unpaved road and onto the blacktop, he started to make real headway. He rounded the corner, jumped the curb, and leaped off his bike in Doc Martin's front yard. He ran up to the door, pounded on it, and rang the doorbell at the same time. "Doctor Martin! Doctor Martin! Help! We need your help!" Ernest called out. Finally the porch light went on. Doc Martin opened the door. "Doctor Martin," Ernest explained, "my mom is going to have the baby. She's at home. We can't get to the hospital. My dad told me to come get you." Doc Martin threw on a jacket and grabbed his medical bag. He and Ernest got in the car and sped off to the Thorpe home.

Karen was watching out the front window when Doc Martin and Ernest pulled in. Mr. Thorpe met them at the door. "I think it's real close now, Doc," he said.

Doc Martin replied, "Well, we'll take a look. You settle down. Everything's going to be all right. We've done this a couple of times already. I'll just need a little help."

Doc Martin asked Ernest and Karen to stay in the living room. It looked like the rain was letting up. He wanted them to keep tabs on it. He and Mr. Thorpe made their way to the bedroom. Mrs. Thorpe was doing her breathing through each contraction. The electricity was still out, so Doc Martin set up several portable lights he had brought along, and Mr. Thorpe found a battery-operated lantern.

Ernest and Karen watched the rain. Finally it stopped. The sky seemed to be getting brighter. Morning was coming. Both Ernest and Karen were getting sleepy. But then they heard a baby crying! A few minutes later Mr. Thorpe walked out of the bedroom, smiling. He sat down with Ernest and Karen and told them, "You have a baby brother. He and Mom are doing great." Mr. Thorpe gave his kids a big hug. He thanked Ernest for getting Doc Martin and Karen for keeping watch at the window. "It wasn't the way we planned it," Mr. Thorpe said, "but we did it together."

"Can we see him, Dad?" Ernest asked.

"Wait a few minutes, and I'll call you in," Mr. Thorpe answered. As Mr. Thorpe went back toward the bedroom, the electricity came on.

Mrs. Thorpe was holding their new son. Doc Martin was packing up his things. When Mr. Thorpe walked in the bedroom and saw the new little life in his wife's arms, he remembered how scary and amazing, how wonderful and miraculous life is. He remembered how it takes your breath away and fills you with joy. He remembered Ernest and Karen. And now, another baby. His eyes filled with tears as he sat next to his wife and their new son.

Mr. Thorpe got up to bring in Ernest and Karen. The doorbell rang. It was Pastor Graff. When the phone went back on, Mrs. Martin called and told him what was going on. He wanted to make sure everything was okay. Mr. Thorpe invited him in and asked him to come along to see the baby. They went in. Ernest and Karen were thrilled. He was so small and so beautiful. Mrs. Thorpe said, "This would be a nice time to say a prayer of thanks."

Pastor Graff read a verse, *"Every good and perfect gift is from above, coming down from the Father of heavenly lights, who does not change like shifting shadows."* Then he prayed: "Gracious Father, today we rejoice in a gift from above, a new little life from You. Thank You. Thank You for this son, who because of Your Son, Jesus, has a future and a life to celebrate. Thank You for this family, which You keep in Your loving care. Thank You for Your good and perfect gifts."

Mr. Thorpe followed with his own prayer as Doc Martin, Ernest, Karen, Pastor Graff, and Mrs. Thorpe bowed their heads: "And Lord, thank You for getting Ernest to Doc Martin's house safely. Thank You for letting Doc Martin be here. You've protected us and blessed us. Thank You for our family and our new son. Amen."

"Amen" was echoed by all. It was a time to give thanks for the gift of a new life.

After the prayer, Mrs. Thorpe asked Pastor Graff where the Bible verse was from. "James 1:17," Pastor Graff replied.

Mrs. Thorpe looked at her husband and said, "Why don't we name him James?" And so it was. The new life, the gift from above on a stormy night, was named James. James Waldon Thorpe. Waldon was a combination of Mrs. Thorpe's father's name, Wallace, and Mr. Thorpe's father's name, Gordon. James Waldon Thorpe, a gift from above.

Mr. Thorpe walked Doc Martin to the door. Pastor Graff went along. They went outside. The sun was breaking through storm clouds lingering on the eastern horizon. "It looks like it's going to be a beautiful day," Doc Martin said. "Be sure to call your doctor in Clare right away," he added. "He'll want to check Mrs. Thorpe and little James. Let your wife get some rest today too. I'll check in on you."

Mr. Thorpe thanked Doc Martin and Pastor Graff once more as they walked to their cars.

Mr. Thorpe went back inside. It had been an amazing summer night and it was a beautiful summer morning. The Lord had given Harrison Town, Michigan, and the Thorpe home another bunch of wonderul gifts. His gifts, from above—the best kind!

GETTING BEHIND

Harrison Town turns out a hearty stock of people. The folks there work hard and play hard. They are an on-the-go bunch. You can't keep them down. You see evidence of that wherever you look. Andy Oreby's father is still in pursuit of the biggest muskie in Budd Lake ever since a 14-year-old girl caught one two pounds heavier than his personal record. Mrs. Parker, who lives in one of the historic homes on Lake Street, has not given up trying to keep kids from cutting across her lawn as they make their way to the Ben Franklin. This year she put a little iron fence on the corner. The kids hurdled it. And then there's Vern Flemming. After wrecking 20 cars, he's working on number 21.

You can't keep them down. That goes for the Thorpe family too, especially Mrs. Thorpe. It was less than a week after the baby was born, but she was determined to have little James baptized on Sunday. She knew it was important. She wanted to give the best she could to her new little son. Mr. Thorpe made sure his wife would still be able to take it easy. After the nine o'clock service at St. Luke, they would host a potluck brunch at their home—

paper plates and minimal cleanup would be the order of the day.

Then Aunt Leona called. Aunt Leona was Mrs. Thorpe's mother's sister. She had good intentions, but sometimes she was a bit too enthusiastic about her preferences. Aunt Leona wanted to see the baby. She told Mrs. Thorpe that she looked great, considering what she had been through. It was amazing that a responsible man like Mr. Thorpe could let a truck battery run down when his wife was pregnant, but she was glad that everything was okay. Of course, the Baptism came up in the conversation, and Aunt Leona wanted to know all the details. What would James wear? What kind of party would follow? Mrs. Thorpe described the family's plan. Aunt Leona just stared at her. "Well, dear," she said, "what *will* the family think? We need to do this right! We want the best for little James. I know a wonderful catering service in Mount Pleasant. It can provide everything you need for a nice brunch. And we'll have to have cake and punch!"

Aunt Leona scanned the Thorpes' yard. "You'll definitely need a tent. You wouldn't want to make everyone squeeze into this tiny house. Better yet, why don't you rent the Legion Hall? Your mother-in-law has an in there, doesn't she?" Before Mrs. Thorpe could get a word in, Aunt Leona stood up to leave. "Oh, this will be a wonderful time. I'm just bubbling over with ideas! If you could give your mother-in-law a call, I'll take care of the rest." And with that Aunt Leona marched out the door.

Wow! Mrs. Thorpe had forgotten how complicated things could get. Was this going to be more work than she had anticipated? She felt like she was already behind.

Mrs. Thorpe mentioned to Mr. Thorpe that Aunt Leona had stopped by to offer her services. Mr. Thorpe excused himself while he went to check whether the dome light in the truck was off. Before they could discuss things, the phone rang. It was Aunt Leona. "I think that church you go to isn't big enough for all of us. I've been calling around to find a bigger church, and I've narrowed it down to two places. By the way," she went on, "I think Ernest and Karen should do some centerpieces for the tables. What do you think of a blue boat in the middle of cotton-candy water? It would be a kind of christening theme, a send-off." Mrs. Thorpe asked Aunt Leona if she could call her back.

After she hung up, Mrs. Thorpe told Ernest about Aunt Leona's centerpiece idea. Ernest excused himself while he went to check whether the dome light in the truck was off. He and his dad came in the house, certain that the dome light was off. And, finally, the Thorpes talked about Baptism plans and Aunt Leona's suggestions. Mr. Thorpe said, "You've got to put a stop to it. Nip it in the bud." Then he looked into his wife's eyes and said, "This is a Baptism. This is our son, the child we prayed for. We need to celebrate what the Lord has done and is doing."

So they devised a plan. Mrs. Thorpe called Aunt Leona and explained that she would receive a postcard invitation. The invitation would outline exactly what would take place on Sunday. Then the Thorpes prepared the invitations:

Come celebrate the Baptism of James Waldon Thorpe, St. Luke Lutheran Church, Harrison

Town, MI, 9:00 A.M. A potluck brunch at the Thorpe home will follow. Please bring a _____

The blank was filled in with a "main dish" or "fruit salad" or "pastry" request. Then Mrs. Thorpe printed at the bottom of each card:

He saved us through the washing of rebirth and renewal by the Holy Spirit, whom He poured out on us generously through Jesus Christ our Savior. Titus 3:5–6

That explained exactly what would take place. Aunt Leona did call, and Mrs. Thorpe said, "Please come. It will be such a nice day." So Aunt Leona did.

So did the other members of the Thorpe family. The church and the overflow area were full. Mrs. Thorpe looked radiant as she cradled little James in her arms. One of Mr. Thorpe's brothers and his wife were sponsors. They were a faithful Christian couple, ready to make a commitment to be spiritual support for little James. Ernest and Karen were dressed up and thrilled about this big day. They watched eagerly as Pastor Graff poured water over the baby's head in the name of the Father and the Son and the Holy Spirit. Mr. Thorpe had tears in his eyes.

The family watched as Pastor Graff got up to preach. The sermon was called "Getting Behind." Pastor Graff talked about how there is a lot to throw you off track in life. "No doubt," he said, "there are plenty of ideas about what is best for little James in life. And there is a lot of pressure to make you feel like you can't keep up or measure up. You're getting behind. That happened to the apostle Peter," Pastor Graff noted. "He had his

147

ideas about Jesus, but Jesus said, 'Get behind me!' Get in line! Go My way! That's what Jesus knew as the best way." Then Pastor Graff talked about the little son who was now in Mr. Thorpe's arms. "The best is what James has received in his Baptism. What's most important for him was given: forgiveness of sins and new life through Jesus. We're put behind Jesus by His grace, and we're brought through death to life!"

Pastor Graff closed his message with some quotes from the Bible. He said, "James is getting behind what's best." He quoted Isaiah 50 and asked these questions: "What can be better than *the word that sustains the weary?* What can be better than *the LORD [who] helps me?* He won't wear out! What can be better than this promise: *Let him who walks in the dark, who has no light, trust in the name of the LORD and rely on his God?* That's what today is all about for little James and for you. Getting behind Jesus is the best place you can be!"

That's just what Mr. and Mrs. Thorpe and everyone in church that day needed to hear. It was a great Baptism day at St. Luke Lutheran Church in Harrison Town, Michigan. Mr. and Mrs. Thorpe were glad they were getting behind with their lives and their family. And at the potluck brunch it seemed that everyone was enjoying and appreciating what they saw and heard that day. Aunt Leona was there too. After she checked the dome light in the truck, she even got to hold the baby. It looked like she was getting behind too—behind Jesus. You can't keep Him down in Harrison Town either.

In the Center

Many fine eateries stand ready to serve their hungry customers in Harrison Town. From the Remedy Restaurant to the Jackpine, from Bucilli's to Tagliamonte's, there are always delightful treats for personal dining pleasure. For those in search of a more casual atmosphere, the new McDonald's, the Dairy Queen, and the Marvel Freeze offer up just the right dish.

Eating opportunities do not end there, however. A quick trip to Clare opens up another array of choices. One of the Thorpes' favorite spots is Ponderosa, a place that accommodates babies quite well.

A supper out for the Thorpe family was long overdue. The buffet and pleasant environment at the Ponderosa in Clare sounded too good to pass up. There was plenty of room for James' baby seat, and the restaurant wasn't too crowded. Ernest and Karen couldn't wait for the all-you-can-eat ice cream.

Then came *the balloon*. Midway into the second helping at the buffet, a waitress brought a red Ponderosa balloon over to James and looped it around the handle on his baby seat. James' eyes fixed right on that balloon. He loved it. It wiggled when he wiggled; he cooed when it bounced gently. Unfortunately, the gentle bouncing loosened the string around the handle on the baby seat. The balloon was airborne. Up it floated next to some air ducts at the top of the vaulted ceiling. Mr. and Mrs. Thorpe, looked at James and watched his face change from delight to despair. He started crying. The waitress heard the commotion, and she brought another balloon, but it was green. She looped it around the handle and told James in a cheerful waitress voice that she had brought another balloon just for him, but the crying continued.

Mr. Thorpe asked the waitress, "Do you have another red one?" They were out of red, she reported. The crying got louder. Mrs. Thorpe picked James up and tried to console him. People stopped eating and looked to see what the problem was. The busboy tried to jump and grab the string of the red balloon. It was no use. James was breaking his own personal volume record. Time to bail out. Mr. Thorpe paid the bill, thanked the waitress and the busboy, and the family left the restaurant. There wasn't even time for all-you-can-eat ice cream. Things sure were different.

The noise didn't stop. For a week after the Ponderosa episode, James decided to cry and wail during suppertime, through bedtime, all the way to three in the morning. Nobody could sleep, and moods were foul. Something had to be done. It was time to see the doctor. After a loud drive back to Clare, James had a thorough going-over by the doctor. "James has no problems at all," the doctor said. "It must be colic."

"What *is* colic?" Mrs. Thorpe asked the doctor. The doctor didn't know. In fact nobody seemed to know. The doctor said it wasn't a problem. The weary Thorpe family didn't agree. Things sure were different.

Fortunately, James settled down as the weeks went by. He even enjoyed small outings with Mom. One favorite place was the grocery store with so many colorful items. The shopping cart was in constant motion. What a great place! Ernest liked it when his mom went shopping too. The IGA had a great selection of potato chips, and this week he requested cheddar and sour cream ripple chips. He couldn't wait until lunchtime! When his mom arrived home, Ernest helped unload the groceries. Mrs. Thorpe settled James back into the house. As Ernest carried in the bags he noticed the diapers and the formula. He found the diaper-rash cream and the baby shampoo. But where were those chips? "Mom," Ernest asked, "where are the cheddar and sour cream …?"

"Oh, no," Mrs. Thorpe replied. "Ernest, I'm sorry. I got sidetracked in the baby section and had to ask a manager to find a rebate coupon. Then James started getting hungry. I forgot your chips." Things sure were different.

Even Sunday evenings got a little different. Mr. Thorpe could see that his wife was tired. She needed a change of scenery. He suggested that they get away for just a half hour of quiet time and have a piece of pie at the Jackpine. That sounded good to Mrs. Thorpe. His parents asked Ernest to watch the baby. They'd be back soon. James was fed and bathed; he had a clean diaper; and he was rocking peacefully in his swing. Mr. and Mrs. Thorpe walked out the door and drove off. That's when Ernest heard a noise coming from the baby swing. Then Ernest smelled something. Ernest thought to himself, No, it can't be. He walked closer to James, who was now stirring around in his swing. He sniffed. "No way," he said out loud. He picked up James and peeked in his diaper. "Oh, no," Ernest sighed. What was he going to do? His parents were going to be gone for 28 more minutes.

"Karen!" Ernest called out. "I've got a job for you!" Karen peeked out of her room, sniffed the air, and closed her bedroom door. This called for planning and ingenuity. Ernest laid James down gently on his changing pad. "I've cornered muskies, caught snakes, and gone through confirmation class," Ernest said to himself. "I can do this." He went into the kitchen and got some towels to wrap his hands in. That didn't work. He took one off and wrapped it over his mouth and nose. Then he saw his mom's dishwashing gloves on the counter. He put them on, got wipes and a diaper ready, held his breath and ... success! Things sure were different.

You see, it wasn't just the routine. It was the constant attention, the awareness, the care, the devotion to that new little guy in the Thorpe home. He was the center of everything!

After Mr. and Mrs. Thorpe came home, she thanked Ernest for his valiant effort and faithful help. Then the family gathered for their devotions. Mr. Thorpe read from Mark 9:30–37:

> They left that place and passed through Galilee. Jesus did not want anyone to know where they were, because He was teaching His disciples. He said to them, "The Son of Man is going to be betrayed into the hands of men. They will kill Him, and after three days

He will rise." But they did not understand what He meant and were afraid to ask Him about it.

They came to Capernaum. When He was in the house, He asked them, "What were you arguing about on the road?" But they kept quiet because on the way they had argued about who was the greatest.

Sitting down, Jesus called the Twelve and said, "If anyone wants to be first, he must be the very last, and the servant of all."

He took a little child and had him stand among them. Taking him in His arms, He said to them, "Whoever welcomes one of these little children in My name welcomes Me; and whoever welcomes Me does not welcome Me but the one who sent Me."

The devotion talked about the difference Jesus made. Because of His care and devotion to us, because of His attention and awareness of our need for forgiveness, things were different now! His life given on the cross brought the forgiveness of sins to our lives in need. He showed that the greatest was measured in terms of servanthood. And with our sins forgiven, with the gift of eternal life, He leads us to be servants too. Things sure are different because of God's love for each one of us. Jesus' life given up for us made that so clear.

That little child caught Ernest's attention. Mr. and Mrs. Thorpe and Karen noticed too. He was in the center. And with that little child in His arms Jesus taught about serving with His love, His love given so freely. Things sure were different for the disciples when they heard that. To be great meant to serve in the way of Jesus, the Savior.

Some great things were happening at the Thorpe home. Little James seemed to be the center of attention. But really Jesus was still at the center, even as life became very different. And when He is in the center, everything *is* different!

VI

STORIES OF A NEW BEGINNING

HE'S NOT HERE

A drive in the country is a wonderful thing to do around Harrison Town as spring arrives and new life explodes into full view. John Batco delighted in his springtime drives. Every morning he climbed into his car and headed for one of the area's more scenic roads. It wasn't traveled much, so Mr. Batco could be assured of a peaceful morning wake-up tour. His route took him down a road that wound slowly around a blind curve to reveal a beautiful vista—majestic pine trees, rocky bluffs, and a valley filled with spring wildflowers. It was his favorite spot.

One morning, as Mr. Batco approached the blind curve, a car suddenly careened around the corner, swung halfway into his lane, and skidded back into its own lane. As the car passed, the teenage driver shouted at him through the open window of his car, *"Pig!"* Mr. Batco laid on his horn and slammed on his brakes. Teenagers! Couldn't they at least behave on Sunday mornings!

Pig! John Batco couldn't believe it. *Pig!* His face turned red. Who was driving like a jerk anyway? What a way to ruin his morning. Teenagers! They were so rude and irresponsible. This was *his* quiet time and *his* special spot. John Batco took a deep breath, pressed the gas pedal, made the turn around that blind curve ... and hit a pig. Right in the middle of the road. A pig. That's what the other driver meant. It looked like John Batco and his mind weren't quite where they should have been.

Mr. Batco wasn't the only one in Harrison Town who was a little out of sync. Ernest Thorpe had a similar problem. It was the week before Easter during his freshman year in high school. Karen, his sister, was ready to color Easter eggs. Ernest had never missed this annual ritual. In fact, he had mastered the art of getting a little bit of each color on an egg without the colors running together. Karen was ready to learn. The six little bowls of dye on the kitchen table were almost ready. The tablets were dissolving, and the vinegary smell filled the kitchen and family room. Karen tugged on Ernest's sleeve. But Ernest mumbled, "Go away. I'm busy." He was sitting on the couch doing nothing.

Karen retreated to the kitchen table and looked at her mom with a "what's wrong with him?" expression on her face. Her mom said quietly, "He's just not here."

This dislocation of Ernest Thorpe was a recent development. The first indication took place a week after Christmas. Ernest's parents got a call from Mr. Tag, Ernest's algebra teacher. A project on some of the great proofs of algebra had been due before Christmas break. Ernest didn't turn his in. Ernest was usually punctual with his assignments. After being questioned by his parents, Ernest found the completed project in his room. Ernest said he just forgot.

It was an isolated incident, the Thorpes thought. After all, there's nothing that compelling about algebraic proofs. Even Mr. Jay didn't seem all that taken by the latest news in algebra. But then something else happened, something a little more compelling.

Valentine's Day was approaching, and it was time for the Valentine's Day Turnabout Cupid Ball held in the Harrison Town High School gymnasium. The girls asked the boys to this one. And Amanda Leeland was the girl Ernest thought would be the ideal Valentine's Day Turnabout Cupid Ball partner. Amanda Leeland was new in town—a petite, dark-haired freshman from the great state of Texas. She moved to Harrison Town with her family after her dad got a job with the county. And when Amanda Leeland said, "Hah, Ernest!" in her sweet Texas drawl, Ernest couldn't help but take a deep breath and swallow.

A few days before the dance the phone rang. "May ah please speak to Ernest, Ma'am?" Amanda asked Mrs. Thorpe. Amanda called to ask Ernest to be her partner at the Valentine's Day Turnabout Cupid Ball. They would be going with two other couples. Amanda's parents had a minivan and her dad would drive. But Ernest said no, he couldn't make it. He was sorry. Then he hung up.

"Ernest," his mom asked, "what's wrong? We would let you go."

But Ernest replied, "Nothing." And that's how it was. He had become a mumbling, eye-rolling, mysterious young teenager.

"He's just not here," his mom said. "He's not here."

The week before Easter Ernest still seemed to be

nowhere. He was going through the motions, doing all the things he was supposed to do. But he didn't seem happy or sad. Just neutral. Easter preparations didn't excite him much at all. When the family left for church early on Easter morning, and Ernest forgot to close the back door, his sister said, "He's *definitely* not here!" Ernest glared at her.

What was it that placed Ernest in this funk? Whatever it was, a change took place on Easter morning. The Thorpe family sat down in church. Ernest ignored the breakfast smells coming from the kitchen. He didn't even peek in or try to snitch a crisp piece of bacon. He just sat in church, staring into space and fidgeting. It was another Easter, another church service. This was the thing to do. More of the same in a life full of the same. At least that was his general outlook until Pastor Graff read the Easter Gospel and followed up with his sermon. In Luke 24:6, the men who sat in the tomb said about Jesus, "He is not here, He has risen!"

"He's not here!" Pastor Graff repeated. *"He's not here!"* Ernest looked straight at him.

"Where are you?" Pastor Graff asked the Easter gathering. "Where are you right now? Waiting for breakfast? Still sleeping? Planning the logistics of your Easter family gathering? How about in life? Where are you? Etched in a schedule book or on a calendar? Pulled around by everyone's plans? Rolling along with the hectic flow of family, job, leisure, and life? Where are you?"

Ernest thought, He's doing it again.

Pastor Graff went on to say that those angels in the tomb of Jesus said, "He's not here!" But that didn't refer to the disappearing trap we fall into so easily. It didn't mean that Jesus stepped out of His activity so He could watch the world go by, go through the motions, go along for the ride. "He's not here" didn't mean that Jesus was nowhere. "He has risen!" the angels declared. And in Mark 16 we're told that He went ahead to Galilee, just as He had told His disciples. Pastor Graff pointed out: "Jesus was somewhere. Right where He promised. He's still somewhere!"

Pastor Graff painted a beautiful picture of the somewhere of Jesus. "We are alive through His victory over death and the grave. The guilt and hurt and condemnation of our sin and failure is forgiven because He sacrificed His life on the cross for us. In Him we find a refuge and strength through it all, until that time of no more death or mourning or crying or pain. Our Savior, Jesus, and His Holy Spirit give to us a life that means something, a life that works! Jesus is somewhere! Right where He promised!"

Pastor Graff looked at the Easter worshipers. Ernest saw him look his way. "And that somewhere," Pastor Graff added, "is where you are this Easter morning! You're no longer covered by the numbing shroud of death. Jesus places you in His somewhere." Pastor Graff said that this somewhere of Jesus was not far away, but was right there, with the people of St. Luke that Easter morning. It was in the Word and in the body and blood of Christ in Communion. Then Pastor Graff challenged the Easter group to remember where they are. He challenged them to resist a nowhere life that can be brought on so easily by our own routine, boredom, distraction, and sin. He challenged them to live in the somewhere of the risen Savior, the great somewhere of the forgiveness of sins, the presence of Jesus, the new life He gives.

Ernest looked around after the Amen. Where had he been? What was he so caught up in that he was missing out on the life God was giving him? How did he get nowhere so quickly? And on Easter morning! It probably was little by little, day by day. But now he was shaken back to the reality of Jesus alive and well. Even for a freshman in high school it was important to be somewhere. Ernest had just heard about the best place to be, and he *was* there.

The Thorpes ate Easter breakfast at church and headed home to prepare for a family gathering that afternoon. There was a difference in Ernest. He helped set the table. He was acting much more like himself. The doorbell rang and Ernest went to answer. He opened the door and found Mr. Leeland, Amanda Leeland, and John Batco. Ernest's mom and dad came to the door and invited the group in. Mr. Leeland explained that Mr. Batco had, unfortunately, collided with a pig on one of the county roads that beautiful Easter morning. On the pig he had found a tag that read "Ernest Thorpe, Clare County Fair, 1992."

That's where that pig went! He had to be somewhere!

Mr. Batco felt responsible for the untimely end of the pig; he wanted to contact any party that might be involved. He knew Mr. Leeland worked for the county. He called Mr. Leeland, who knew Ernest because of his daughter Amanda, who was in the same class as Ernest at Harrison Town High School. She came along to say hello.

Mr. and Mrs. Thorpe thanked Mr. Batco for his concern. And they thanked Mr. Leeland for his work above and beyond the call of duty, especially on Easter morning. They looked at Ernest with wonder in their eyes about that pig! Then Ernest asked if Amanda could stay for dinner. She could. It looked like Ernest was back to his old self again—make that his *new* self.

Yes, it would have been easy to be nowhere that Easter Day in Harrison Town, Michigan. But the good news is that Jesus puts you somewhere, and it is worth staying in that somewhere with Him. Ernest walked up to his mom, gave her a hug, and said something that you can say on Easter and every day because of Jesus, who lives, "I'm back!"

THE TRUTH

When Easter arrived in Harrison Town everyone knew that spring was just around the corner. Sometimes the winter days hung on a little too long, but this year was different. Brown and bare winterized woods surrendered to green grass, crocuses, tulips, and daffodils. And the birds! They were crossing central Michigan on their spring migration. Some lingered for the warm weather that followed in their wake.

That meant bird-watching! The Harrison Town Bird-Watching Society gathered at strategic points along the shore of Budd Lake. The members rose before sunrise, braved the chilly temperatures, got soaked as they hiked through the dew-covered woods, with no guarantee of success.

Bird-watching is a wonderful hobby, as well as a fresh-air, creation-appreciating, educational one. But for Ernest Thorpe and the rest of his class, bird-watching generated only animosity toward their fine feathered friends. This dislike of birds, according to Ernest, was caused by their biology teacher, who was a bird-watching fanatic! Her name was Mrs. Eggold. Really! Mrs.

Robin Eggold. Her parents must have known. That's like the driver's education teacher named Mr. Carr. Very strange coincidences. Mrs. Eggold went on and on in class about her latest avifaunal adventures. She urged the class to get up far too early on Saturday mornings so they too could be enriched by spotting the latest specimen. She let them know that their lives would be incomplete without a detailed personal bird identification log. She urged them to purchase her *Personal Field Guide for the Birds of North America,* available in the school bookstore. "No bird-watcher worth her binoculars ever goes on a birding expedition without it," she said. And she said it over and over again, especially at this time of year.

It was a relief for Ernest to get home after an intense bird day at school. He had enough. Paul Tucker and Ernest planned to spend the afternoon together. They would do some homework, eat supper, and close out the evening with some team Nintendo. Part of the evening at the Thorpe home also included family devotion time. After supper Mr. Thorpe read from the Bible and a devotion book. That evening he read a post-Easter devotion from John 20, the account of Thomas:

Now Thomas (called Didymus), one of the Twelve, was not with the disciples when Jesus came. So the other disciples told him, "We have seen the Lord!"

But he said to them, "Unless I see the nail marks in His hands and put my finger where the nails were, and put my hand into His side, I will not believe it."

165

A week later His disciples were in the house again, and Thomas was with them. Though the doors were locked, Jesus came and stood among them and said, "Peace be with you!" Then He said to Thomas, "Put your finger here; see My hands. Reach out your hand and put it into My side. Stop doubting and believe."

Thomas said to Him, "My Lord and my God!"

Then Jesus told him, "Because you have seen Me, you have believed; blessed are those who have not seen and yet have believed."

Jesus did many other miraculous signs in the presence of His disciples, which are not recorded in this book. But these are written that you may believe that Jesus is the Christ, the Son of God, and that by believing you may have life in His name.

The devotion talked about the *truth*. Thomas wondered whether Jesus really was alive. But Jesus showed the *truth*. And the truth lasts. Truth gets talked about and causes a stir in life. Thomas said, "My Lord and my God!" Throughout history innumerable others have said the same thing. The truth lasts, and it causes a stir in one's life. The Bible reading said that "these are written that you may believe that Jesus is the Christ, the Son of God, and that by believing you may have life in His name." That's the purpose of the truth of Jesus—the forgiveness of sins, life everlasting. The news of Jesus the Savior lasts because it's the truth! Followers and believers live it and talk about it. It changes lives. It's the truth!

Mr. Thorpe closed out the devotion with a prayer. Ernest and Paul were excused to pursue their Nintendo interests. That devotion, however, stuck in Ernest's mind. "The truth lasts," he mumbled to Paul Tucker. "It causes a stir in life."

"What?" Paul asked. "What are you talking about, Ernest?"

"I was just thinking about Mrs. Eggold," Ernest replied. "What if she spotted a rare bird right here in Harrison Town? Wouldn't that cause a stir?"

"She would go crazy!" Paul answered. "It would be fun to cause that stir!"

"Yeah, it sure would," Ernest added in a thoughtful way. "Why don't *we* make sure she sees one?"

And so, the plot was hatched. Ernest and Paul looked through Mrs. Eggold's "Wish List of Birds to Spot" on page 327 of her *Personal Field Guide for the Birds of North America*. They found the perfect bird: a black-backed, three-toed woodpecker. It was an "uncommon woodpecker even in its preferred habitat—coniferous forests." Its call was a sharp "pik." It was the perfect bird to cause a stir. Paul would do the artwork. He made a wooden woodpecker about eight inches long and painted it to look just like the black-backed, three-toed woodpecker. Ernest would lead Mrs. Eggold to the wonderful bird.

Ernest discovered that the Harrison Town Bird-Watching Society—and Mrs. Eggold—would be staking out the island in Budd Lake on Saturday morning. Their vantage point was an onshore location west of the island but close enough to observe any fowl activity. A perfect setup, Ernest thought. The pine trees on the island were

167

a perfect habitat for the black-backed, three-toed woodpecker. Ernest would go with the bird-watching group, and Paul would operate the bird on the island. All he had to do was row to the island from the east—a very short distance, set up the bird discreetly in a pine tree, and hide.

Early Saturday morning the hunt was on. Mrs. Eggold led the group of bird enthusiasts down to Budd Lake. She was thrilled that Ernest Thorpe had taken an interest in bird pursuits! He even had the motivation to get up before sunrise on a Saturday. He was a rare species of a teenager, to be sure. While triumphant thoughts of a conversion ran through Mrs. Eggold's head, another rare species—or a facsimile thereof—was set up by Paul Tucker in viewing range of the birding group. Paul tied some fishing line to the bird so he could pull it off the side of the pine tree. A fleeting view would be more of a tease. He would listen for the black-backed, three-toed woodpecker call from Mrs. Eggold, and down the fraudulent feathered friend would come!

As the sun rose, the bird-watchers quietly surveyed the island. The great blue heron was in town. A kingfisher was spotted. A Baltimore oriole made an appearance. Then Ernest peered through his binoculars and asked innocently, "Mrs. Eggold, what's that one with yellow on its head?"

"Where?" Mrs. Eggold shot back.

"In that pine tree." Ernest tried not to grin.

Mrs. Eggold looked. Her mouth opened wide. "It can't be," she said. "This far south is such a rare sighting! Maybe it's the mild spring or the harsh winter," she reasoned to herself. Then Mrs. Eggold spoke to the group,

"Fellow bird enthusiasts, we have located a black-backed, three-toed woodpecker! It has never been seen here in Harrison Town before!" All binoculars focused on the pine tree to get a glimpse while Mrs. Eggold tried her black-backed, three-toed woodpecker call. As soon as it came out of her mouth, the bird disappeared. Good job, Paul, Ernest thought. The trick worked!

The sighting caused quite a stir. Not only did Mrs. Eggold call the *Clare County Cleaver*, which promised front-page coverage, she also informed the district bird-watching society's grand birder. And how she went on and on in biology class on Monday! Since this was such a rare find, and since the migratory period might last only a week, Mrs. Eggold was scheduling a special field trip for early Wednesday morning. A *Clare County Cleaver* photographer would be there to take pictures for the Thursday edition. Bird-watching groups from around the state were being bused in.

Wow. This *was* a stir! All over a bird! Paul and Ernest looked at each other as Mrs. Eggold spoke. What were they going to do? The bird had to show up now. They didn't want Mrs. Eggold to be a laughingstock. Paul would have to put the bird back in the tree.

Buses of bird-watchers streamed into town. Mrs. Eggold was beaming. And the male "Picoides articus"—the black-backed, three-toed woodpecker—would show up again. Paul Tucker was ready on Wednesday. He got up very early, snuck over to the island in Budd Lake, and placed the bird on the pine tree. It was chilly that morning. Paul's shoes were wet from his walk across the island and from stepping into Budd Lake when he got out of the boat. He peered out from behind a rock to see the crowds gathering as the sun rose. Then Paul Tucker couldn't hold back. He tried as hard as he could, but he was shivering and cold. "Ah, ah, ahhh ... choo!" Paul let out a very loud sneeze. Birds flew in every direction. The bird enthusiasts gasped. Ernest winced. When Paul sneezed, he pulled the fake woodpecker from its perch in the pine tree. Now it dangled from a branch. Every set of binoculars focused on the rare bird. They watched a panicky boy grab a black-backed, three-toed woodpecker off a pine branch and run from sight.

Ernest put his head in his hands. The bird crowd began to disperse. "Ernest," Mrs. Eggold asked, "did I see Paul Tucker running away with a fake bird in his hand?" Ernest confessed. Of course, there wasn't much to confess. The truth was pretty clear. The truth lasts. It has lasting effects and causes more than a temporary stir.

No crime was committed, but Mrs. Eggold and the Thorpe and Tucker parents agreed that a long term paper on rare bird species in North America would be a fitting consequence of the bird fakery. In addition, each of the boys wrote an apology to the bird-watching organizations of the area as well as to the *Clare County Cleaver.* Nintendo was nixed too—for the rest of the school year.

The truth would have been better. Ernest and Paul saw that clearly. There is something about the truth that keeps working and does good things. "These are written," the apostle John wrote, "that you may believe that Jesus is the Christ, the Son of God, and that by believing you may have life in His name." That's the truth of Jesus. Can it cause a lasting and wonderful stir in your life? It's supposed to! And it does last!

MAKING NOISE

The month of May brings excitement and activity to everyone's life. Things are growing; grass needs mowing. Families are gathering; big events are happening. One such event is confirmation day. Confirmation Sunday at St. Luke was filled with commotion, excitement, families, picture-taking, and crowds. What a great time for the young people who would make public confirmation of their faith in their Savior, Jesus.

Ernest Thorpe was confirmed last year and was just a bystander this year. Pastor Graff began his message in good attention-getting fashion. He talked about noise and the effect noise has on us. He told the story of a young pastor preaching a wonderful sermon. He wanted to do his best for the members of his congregation. So when a baby started crying during his sermon, he overlooked it and kept preaching. Finally the mother of the child stood up with her little one and began to walk out of church. The pastor stopped preaching. He said to the mother, "You don't have to leave. The baby isn't bothering me."

The woman turned to the pastor and said, "That's not the problem. You're bothering him!"

Yes, noise affects different people in different ways. All this talk about noise got Ernest thinking about noise in his life. One of his favorite classes at school was study hall with Mr. Buchmann. He was the one who helped to make it a favorite for Ernest and most everybody else. Because of a staff shortage at the school, Mr. Buchmann had to leave the room on a regular basis. And when he left, the fun began! Hockey tournaments with wadded-up balls of paper; paper-airplane flying contests; field-goal competitions with paper footballs. And the talk! It was a real free-for-all, let-your-hair-down, put-your-feet-up, and do-anything-you-want time. That's why Ernest liked it.

What about getting caught? That was the beauty of the class and of Mr. Buchmann himself. You see, Mr. Buchmann *made noise*. He rattled and jingled and squeaked when he walked. He must have had five dollars worth of change in his pocket at all times. In addition, he wore one of those key rings with an extendable chain on his belt. It looked like every key for every door in the school district was hanging from that key ring. Then there were his shoes, which let out two telling squeaks with every step. There was the low, quick squeak and then the longer sliding-up-the-scale squeak. With change rattling, keys jangling, and shoes squeaking you could hear Mr. Buchmann coming a mile away—and definitely from down the hallway and around the corner. Ernest's study-hall friends had organized rotating lookouts—or *listenouts*. When the lookout heard Mr. Buchmann he signaled the class, the groups dispersed, all contraband was hidden, and books were placed in appropriate positions. Mr. Buchmann looked in the room, then headed back to his other task down the hall and around the corner. Then the festivities resumed. Mr. Buchmann checked the class only once or twice in a 50-minute period, so there was a lot of quality goofing-off for Ernest and the rest of his cohorts.

That was the noise that drifted fondly into Ernest's mind when Pastor Graff brought up the subject. Ernest almost laughed out loud when Pastor Graff asked, "What kind of noise do the people in your life make?" Pastor Graff talked about confirmation Sunday noises. He talked about the Scripture readings and the hymns, the confirmation vows, and the words of Jesus in Holy Communion. He talked about the confirmation sermon. Ernest really didn't remember any of those things from his confirmation day.

Then Pastor Graff talked about the noise of family celebrations. He mentioned the noise of confirmation students who say, "It's over!" and "I wonder what I'll get for confirmation!" Ernest remembered that noise, and he remembered that he got some money, clothes from an aunt, a new generator light set for his bike, and a great video game.

Pastor Graff pointed out that those are wonderful noises, but the point of confirmation is hearing and making the right noise. Reading from Acts 13, Pastor Graff quoted St. Paul, who stood up and said to the people in Pisidian Antioch, "Men of Israel and you Gentiles who worship God, listen to me!"

"Paul went on to make some important noise," Pastor Graff continued. "He talked about the history of God's care for His people through the ages. Then he spoke about Jesus, who fulfilled God's promise of a Savior for us from sin and death, who was raised from the dead and seen by so many."

Pastor Graff quoted St. Paul's words in Acts 13:38 as one of the greatest noises ever heard, "Therefore, my brothers, I want you to know that through Jesus the forgiveness of sins is proclaimed to you."

That's the noise of confirmation. Pastor Graff noted that each confirmation student has had his or her ears opened to the noise of Jesus, the beautiful noise of the Good Shepherd who said, "My sheep listen to My voice; I know them, and they follow Me. I give them eternal life, and they shall never perish; no one can snatch them out of My hand. My Father, who has given them to Me, is greater than all; no one can snatch them out of My Father's hand. I and the Father are one."

Forgiveness of sins and eternal life, a Savior who is strong and caring—that's the noise God makes in our lives because He loves us.

As Ernest heard the words and looked at the white-robed confirmation group up front, he started to remember that noise for his life.

Then Pastor Graff talked about doing some noise-making! He asked the confirmation class what noise they were going to make as people who have been baptized into Christ's name and who confess Him to be their Savior and Lord. You could see Pastor Graff's eyes meet each one of his student's eyes as he asked the question. Making the noise of Jesus was a big responsibility at home, at school, and everywhere they went. Ernest remembered that responsibility. He thought about the year that had passed since confirmation. He thought about Jesus' noise that made a difference coming through his life.

Pastor Graff closed out by challenging everyone there, and especially the confirmation class, to be noisy people with the noise of Jesus Christ. That was noise that made a difference and had a purpose. It was noise you could work at.

Ernest hadn't expected to hear so much. He thought it was over for him. But now he knew he was still at an important beginning. This *was* good noise for him to hear. After the service was over, Ernest stood with his family as they waited to leave the church. People were talking and laughing and taking pictures. Ernest felt a tap on his shoulder. He turned around and saw Mr. Buchmann!

"Mr. Buchmann, I didn't hear you coming!"

Ernest winced with regret. That really slipped out quickly. But Mr. Buchmann replied, "Oh, I use all that change, those keys, and those terrible squeaky shoes for study hall. I figure when the kids hear me coming they'll shape up. And it works!"

Hmmm. Making noise with a purpose. Noise that made a difference.

Mr. Buchmann went on, "I have a nephew in the confirmation class, and I saw you standing here. I just wanted to say hello and tell you that you have a nice church. I could really relate to that sermon too."

Ernest thanked Mr. Buchmann, who turned and walked away *without a sound*.

Making noise for a reason. Mr. Buchmann was on the right track. After hearing the right noise of Jesus, and being challenged to make that noise, maybe the confirmation students were on the right track too that confirmation Sunday. Ernest was.

YOU CAN TELL

. . . .

It was another beautiful spring day in Harrison Town. The warm sun helped the temperature climb into the pleasant range. The sky was clear and vivid blue. Young green leaves filled the trees. Budd Lake looked more inviting than it had in a long time. To make the day even more special, it was Mother's Day. Gatherings, corsages, meals, and outings defined the order of the day. While Mother's Day was wonderful, one day was not always the right medicine for a weary mother.

Mrs. Thorpe knew that in a big way. She had a teenager, Ernest. With his feverish pace, his moods that seemed to change as quickly as little James' diapers, and his spirit of independence, he was a tiring young man to keep up with. Then there was Karen, a delightful first grader. But room-mother duties, school projects, class needs, field trips, and homework did their fair share to run Mrs. Thorpe even more ragged. And then came little James, only nine months old. His diaper changes occurred as often as Ernest's mood changes. Did I mention that already? With bottles and car seats and naps and crawling all around the house, Mrs. Thorpe was one burnt-out mom. There hadn't been a break since August.

So one day in the year, Mother's Day, just wasn't enough!

Mr. Thorpe saw that. He knew his wife needed a break. So before Mother's Day, as a combination Mother's Day and anniversary present, Mr. Thorpe surprised her with a wonderful gift—a three-day cruise in the balmy waters between Florida and the Bahamas. They would fly down the Thursday before Mother's Day, float and relax on Friday, Saturday, and Sunday, and head home on Monday. Mr. Thorpe arranged for his mother to come for the weekend to watch the kids. Mrs. Thorpe was thrilled! A Mother's Day weekend cruise. Rest and relaxation. No cooking or cleaning. Just the big job of soaking in some sun. What mother wouldn't go for that?

For Ernest that meant a weekend on his own! Sure Grandma Thorpe would be there, but she would be tending the little ones. He would be free! No one would bug him about cleaning his room. No one would bug him to eat everything on his plate. No one would bug him to do his homework. No one would bug him to stop playing video games. This would be all right!

Thursday afternoon came. Mr. and Mrs. Thorpe packed their suitcases and kissed their children good-bye. Karen asked when they were coming back. James drooled. Ernest went into his room and turned on the radio—a little louder than regulation.

Friday turned out to be okay. It was a school day. Mrs. Thorpe had made their school lunches in advance, and Grandma Thorpe took the kids to McDonald's for supper.

But then Saturday came. Things were a little different. When Ernest woke up he didn't smell breakfast. Usually his mom prepared something special for Saturday breakfast—pancakes or bacon and eggs. And it didn't really matter to him as he lay there this Saturday morning before Mother's Day, but it was also customary for his mom to come into his room, give him a kiss, and tell him what special treat she had made. Ernest got out of bed, went into the kitchen, and found Grandma feeding James. She whipped up some oatmeal for Ernest and Karen—which was fine, even though it wasn't like their mom usually made. But it was a day of freedom! Ernest cut the grass and then went bike riding with Paul Tucker. As Paul and Ernest raced home, Paul said, "Hey, our finish line flags aren't up!" Mrs. Thorpe hung the laundry out on nice Saturdays. Paul and Ernest could usually see the sheets blowing in the breeze as they rode up the street. They would accelerate and race all the way to that finish line. As the boys pulled into Ernest's driveway, Paul said, "You sure can tell your mom is gone."

"Yeah," Ernest answered, "you can tell."

Sunday arrived. Pastor Graff preached a Mother's Day sermon. Moms were gathered with their families. But no mom for Ernest. Oh, it was fine that Grandma was there, but things were different. There were no jokes from Mom on the way home, no commentary on the sermon or questions about Sunday school. And the "no Nintendo until after lunch" request was conspicuously absent. Ernest didn't even play it that Sunday. He just thought about Paul Tucker's comment, "You sure can tell your mom is gone."

That evening Mr. and Mrs. Thorpe called. Everybody got to talk—even James. Mr. and Mrs. Thorpe told all about the fun they were having. Their room was nice. The food was amazing! From complete breakfast spreads to fancy dinners to remarkable midnight buffets—it was like a dream! They described walks around the deck in the evening, watching the sunrise in the morning, and the beautiful weather. They talked about the entertainment, the activities, and the shops. They found out that the ship's captain was from a town in Michigan not far from Harrison Town, and after they introduced themselves, they got an invitation to come up to the bridge and even sit at the captain's table for dinner! What a wonderful time! "How is everything going there?" they asked.

"Just fine, great," Ernest answered.

Finally, Monday rolled around. After school Karen was coloring in her room, James was napping, and Ernest was sulking. Grandma Thorpe walked into the family room and sat down next to him. "Ernest," she asked, "what's on your mind?"

"Hair," he answered. Both he and Grandma laughed. That was one of Mom's jokes. Then Ernest got serious. "Mom and Dad really love each other. You can tell," Ernest said.

"That's true," Grandma replied. "It's not that way in every family. You're blessed, Ernest."

Then Ernest got to what was really on his mind. "I know that one day I'll have to leave," Ernest explained. "I sure hope I can find someone like Mom."

"You can, Ernest. You can."

"What makes Mom so special? Why does she put up with all the work around here? It would be much nicer to be on a cruise, wouldn't it?"

Grandma Thorpe put her arm around her grandson. "Ernest," she said, "your mother loves you, and your mother loves the Lord and what He has given her to do. You are God's gifts to her and she knows that. God has taken care of her in so many amazing ways. Jesus gave His life for her. Your mom holds that very precious and wants to pass on that love. Jesus even said, 'Love one another. As I have loved you, so you must love one another.' Your mom wants the best for you. She loves you, and she loves her Savior. That's what makes her so special."

"You can tell," Ernest said. "How can I find someone like that?" Ernest was thinking about girls. He was thinking about being popular in high school. He was also thinking about life in the future and the special life he had now.

"Ernest, there are no fancy tricks. It's not what you have or how much attention you can get. If you love the Lord and show love like He's shown you, someone will be able to tell that you're special, that you can love and show care."

Ernest understood something special that Mother's Day weekend. It was something he didn't want missing from his life—the unique and lasting love of God Himself through Jesus and through his mom.

Monday evening arrived, and no one missed the sound of the truck pulling into the driveway. Mom and Dad were home! They arrived to a fanfare of baby cries, hugs, kisses, and smiles. What a welcome! Flowers were in a vase on the kitchen counter as a belated present for Mrs. Thorpe. The kids picked them just for her, Grandma told Mrs. Thorpe. Mom and Dad looked tan and refreshed. After the rousing welcome and the handing out of cruise souvenirs, Mr. Thorpe turned to his wife and said, "They really missed us. You can tell!"

Grandma Thorpe looked at her son and daughter-in-law and remarked, "More than you know." For Mr. and Mrs. Thorpe, on a long Mother's Day weekend, it was good to be away. But for a faithful Mom and Dad in the care of a Savior who loved them so much, it was also good to come home.

BUT NOT AFRAID

Grass-cutting was in full swing in Harrison Town. Flowers—petunias, begonias, marigolds—were planted in freshly hoed beds. Tomato, pepper, and cucumber plants were still small and tender. The raspberry plants were growing well. Budd Lake remained a bit too chilly for fishing, but the signs of life were everywhere. The anticipation of summer was running high. Everything was normal in Harrison Town.

On a sunny Sunday afternoon Grandma and Grandpa Thorpe were at the Thorpe home. Every spring Grandma came to help Mr. and Mrs. Thorpe put in their bedding plants. Mr. Thorpe did the digging and the hoeing, and Grandma and Mrs. Thorpe did the planting. Ernest cut the grass, and Grandpa went on walks with Karen. Hand in hand they went down the road, by the woods, to a little pond west of the house. Karen was Grandpa's special friend. She looked forward to these walks and asked questions about what she saw. Grandpa taught her about the woods and the world. They talked about everything. On that sunny Sunday afternoon they had a great time, as usual.

But the phone ringing after midnight was not usual. It was Grandma. Grandpa was being rushed to the hospital. It was his heart again. Mr. Thorpe left right away. Mrs. Thorpe said a prayer with the children and waited at home for an update.

In the morning Grandpa was stable. Ernest and Karen went to school. Mrs. Thorpe took James with her and drove to the hospital in Clare. Grandpa was in the cardiac care unit. He was hooked up to all kinds of monitors. It was hard to see Grandpa Thorpe so sick and to see Grandma Thorpe there at his side, so concerned about her husband. They had been married for 61 years. No one could comprehend the memories they shared or imagine the life they had walked through together—the first time they saw each other after the war; the songs they danced to; the energy and vigor they had while raising 13 children; their hopes and happiness; their disappointments and hard times. No one knew them as completely as they knew each other. And to see the person you love in such difficulty was hard.

Grandma and Grandpa Thorpe's pastor arrived. He read Grandpa's confirmation verse, John 14:27: " 'Jesus said, 'Peace I leave with you; My peace I give you. I do not give to you as the world gives. Do not let your hearts be troubled and do not be afraid.' "

The pastor prayed with Grandma and Grandpa. Just as they finished, the doctor came in. Because of Grandpa's swelling they would have to cut off his wedding ring. Grandpa never took that ring off. As the ring came off, Grandma and Grandpa Thorpe cried.

The night didn't go well for Grandpa Thorpe. The doctors could do nothing more. All of the family gathered at the hospital. At eight o'clock that evening Grandpa Thorpe died. He was 81. Two of his children couldn't get there—Mr. Thorpe's oldest brother and one sister. They felt bad that they arrived after their father died, but the family comforted them.

Everything happened so fast in the days that followed. There were funeral arrangements, arrangements for flowers, the obituary, the visitation, the funeral, and the burial. It was too fast.

At the funeral, Grandma and Grandpa Thorpe's pastor tried to slow things down. He read Jesus' words in John 14:27 again, "Peace I leave with you; My peace I give you. I do not give to you as the world gives. Do not let your hearts be troubled and do not be afraid." He read Psalm 23 and from Revelation 21:

> I saw the Holy City, the new Jerusalem, coming down out of heaven from God, prepared as a bride beautifully dressed for her husband. And I heard a loud voice from the throne saying, "Now the dwelling of God is with men, and He will live with them. They will be His people, and God Himself will be with them and be their God. He will wipe every tear from their eyes. There will be no more death or mourning or crying or pain, for the old order of things has passed away."

The pastor talked about the peace Jesus gives and about the life in heaven that Grandpa had now—perfect peace. For Grandpa and for everyone at that funeral service, that is the reason Jesus came. That is why He died on the cross and why He forgives us. To give peace, real and lasting peace, through life and even through death. It is the peace of heaven, the peace of a wonderful reunion there. It is the peace of knowing that Grandpa was okay and alive with Jesus. It is the peace of knowing they would be okay too, because Jesus cared for them. What else could slow things down and give such comfort like that great news?

After the funeral, the family gathered at Grandma and Grandpa's house. It was packed with friends and family. People were eating and talking. As Grandma Thorpe walked around and surveyed the situation, she received warm greetings and hugs and sympathy from everyone. But Grandma couldn't spot Karen. Where could she be? After checking outside, where the rest of the grandchildren were, Grandma looked in the house. She found Karen in the bedroom, crying. Grandma sat down on the bed next to her granddaughter.

"Grandpa was your special friend, wasn't he, Karen?"

Karen nodded her head. "I wish I could see him again," Karen said tearfully.

"Oh, Karen, you will. You'll see him in heaven. So will I. That's why Jesus rose from the dead, so we can too."

"Is he there right now? Does he go there right away?" Karen asked.

"He sure is," replied Grandma. "Just as the angels carried poor Lazarus to heaven, they carried Grandpa there too."

"Is Grandpa an angel?" Karen inquired.

"No," Grandma replied. "Angels are angels. People are people. Grandpa is just himself."

"Is he lonely there? Is it boring in heaven?" Karen was concerned.

"Oh, no, Karen," Grandma explained. "It's a beautiful place, better than the best place you can think of. Grandpa's got lots of friends in heaven. His mom and dad are there too. And, of course, Jesus is with him. He's not lonely. And he'll never be bored or sad."

"Do you think he misses me?" Karen asked.

Grandma answered, "Oh, I'm sure He would love to hold your hand and go on a walk with you right now, but as long as Jesus is with you and Jesus is with Grandpa, then you're still together."

"Can Grandpa talk to Noah?" Karen asked.

"I suppose he can," Grandma replied.

"How about Mary and Joseph?"

"I suppose he can talk to them too. That sounds pretty neat, doesn't it?" Grandma asked Karen.

Karen agreed and asked, "Why can't I go there right now?"

Grandma smiled. "It's not time for you to go there yet. God wants you to be here to help Him still. God needs you here."

"Good," Karen answered. "I like it here."

"God wants you to like it here," said Grandma.

"Grandma, why do people die? Why do bad things happen?"

"The world is a hurting place, Karen," Grandma answered with the best answer she could give. "God didn't make it a hurting place. We did. So now we need His help. And Jesus came to help us. Now we're here to bring His help to more people. And one day, Jesus will come to make it all better."

Karen paused. Then she asked, "Are you sad, Grandma?"

"Yes," Grandma said. She put her arm around Karen.

"I'll miss Grandpa," Karen added.

"Me too," Grandma said. "But you don't have to be afraid. This is what we need to be ready for. Jesus is with us through it all."

Then Karen asked, "Grandma, will you take walks with me?"

"I sure will. We'll need each other. We both miss Grandpa."

Grandma Thorpe and Karen gave each other a big hug. They wiped away their tears, stood up, and walked out of the bedroom hand in hand. As they left, Grandma turned to look at the black-and-white wedding picture of her and her husband on the dresser. Then she and Karen went out to join the others. They were sad but not afraid. By the grace of God, through the peace of Jesus, they were not afraid.

WHOM TO BELIEVE

P art of the annual excitement at the end of the school year was spring sports. The high school in Harrison Town was ready to accommodate that excitement with a beautiful new track, financed by generous donations. The fenced-in track surrounded the football field.

It was a great track, and track is just what Ernest Thorpe happened to be was interested in. He liked to run, but he had no team experience. Yet the notice posted on the activity board caught Ernest's eye. A meeting for all those interested in the Harrison Town Hornet boys track squad would be held tomorrow during lunch hour. Ernest decided to check it out.

You should have seen the guys at that meeting! There were big guys; there were fast guys; there were guys who knew all about all the events. And when Ernest Thorpe, a small freshman, walked into that room, the big track veterans seemed to stare and snicker. The coach didn't pay any attention to Ernest either. After discussing tryouts, workouts, splits, spikes, and stretching, the coach handed out the tryout schedule for a week from Friday, after school, at the new track. Ernest left the meeting thinking, *There is no way I'm going out for track! Why even try?*

After school Ernest told his friend Andy Oreby about the meeting. Andy had the same reaction. "Why even think about it, Ernest?"

Ernest talked to Paul Tucker too. "Get out of here!" Paul said. "Why did you even go to that meeting?"

Ernest was now even more resolute in his decision. "Why should I try out? Why did I think I could even do that?" Ernest asked himself.

But that thought would soon be challenged. The next day at school, Ernest saw a familiar face. It was Michael, the guy at the Fellowship of Christian Athletes table at freshman registration. Ernest still had his FCA brochure at home. "Hey, Ernest, remember me?" Michael asked. Ernest said he did, and Michael went on. "I saw you at the track meeting yesterday. I'm glad you're interested! We've got an FCA track preparation meeting tomorrow after school. Do you want to stop by?"

Uh-oh. More pressure. Ernest felt uncomfortable. Why did he even think about track? So Ernest replied, "Uh, I don't know."

Michael was persistent, "Stop by study hall after school tomorrow. We're going to get ready for a great track season!" Ernest nodded his head, and Michael walked down the hall to his next class. What was Ernest being dragged in to now? That night all he could do was toss and turn.

Ernest awoke with a renewed lack of self-confidence. "No way," he said. "I'm not going to any more meetings. I'm going to school, then I'm coming home. Why even think about track? It's impossible. I can't do it." Ernest got through the whole day without one close encounter of the track kind. The final bell rang, and he was free! He couldn't believe it! Ernest made his way happily down the hallway toward the exit. Then he heard a familiar voice.

"Hey, Ernest, I'm glad you hung around for the meeting!" It was Michael. They turned the corner into study hall—one doorway before the exit.

When Ernest walked into the study hall, he was surprised. Many of the same big guys who were at the track meeting were there. They even said hello. Michael welcomed all newcomers to the Fellowship of Christian Athletes track preparation meeting. He said the purpose of the meeting was to get spiritually pumped and prepared for tryouts and the season. Michael opened with a prayer and reading from John 17:20–23. It was Jesus' prayer for believers:

> I pray also for those who will believe in Me through [My disciples'] message, that all of them may be one, Father, just as You are in Me and I am in You. May they also be in Us so that the world may believe that You have sent Me. I have given them the glory that You gave Me, that they may be one as We are one: I in them and You in Me. May they be brought to complete unity to let the world know that You sent Me and have loved them even as You have loved Me.

Michael talked about track being more than just a

school-team opportunity. It was also a Christian-team opportunity. Since Jesus is in us, we show Him in all we do. Track was another opportunity to show the love and self-sacrifice of Jesus, who gave His life to forgive us. Track talent was a way of glorifying Him. Sportsmanship was one way to show that the love and life Christ gives works.

Ernest thought that was great to hear. He was pleasantly surprised that this good news could be heard in one of his high school classrooms. But he still had his doubts about track. The guys at the meeting were big. The coach didn't seem to care. Even his friends were convinced that making the team was an impossible dream.

After the meeting Michael said, "So, Ernest, are you going to try out?"

Ernest had to answer honestly. He couldn't hide it any more. "No way," he said. "Why should I? It's useless." Ernest explained all the reasons that made it logical for him to fail at track.

Michael listened patiently, then he replied, "Ernest, the question you should ask is, 'Why *shouldn't* I?' Why not try out? You heard what Jesus said. He is in you! Jesus didn't make you to fade into the woodwork. Who are you going to believe, friends who doubt you, a coach's scowl, or Jesus? *Why not try*, Ernest?" Then Michael added, "Besides, I saw you running around. You look like a strong runner. I think you have some talent. I'll tell you what, I'll give you some secret weapons. Think about it, and pray about it, and I'll ask you tomorrow." Ernest agreed. Michael wrote down two Bible references on a piece of paper, Isaiah 40:28–31 and Hebrews 12:1–2. "Look these up," Michael said. "They're secret weapons."

That evening Ernest opened his Bible and looked up the passages. Isaiah 40:28–31 read this way:

> Do you not know? Have you not heard? The LORD is the everlasting God, the Creator of the ends of the earth. He will not grow tired or weary, and His understanding no one can fathom. He gives strength to the weary and increases the power of the weak. Even youths grow tired and weary, and young men stumble and fall; but those who hope in the LORD will renew their strength. They will soar on wings like eagles; they will run and not grow weary, they will walk and not be faint.

Wow! What a great verse! Then Ernest checked Hebrews 12:1–2:

> Therefore, since we are surrounded by such a great cloud of witnesses, let us throw off everything that hinders and the sin that so easily entangles, and let us run with perseverance the race marked out for us. Let us fix our eyes on Jesus, the author and perfecter of our faith.

Another great secret weapon! Ernest prayed and thought. Why not? Why not try? Why not?

The next day Ernest caught up with Michael. Michael asked, "Well, Ernest, what do you think?"

Ernest answered, "Why not!" He went into the coach's office and signed up. The coach gave him a try-out training sheet. Ernest started running. He lifted some weights and did some stretching. After all, why not? Make the team or not, everything would be okay.

Michael and his friends even invited Ernest to go along on some runs after school. Ernest did not finish last.

It was a quick push to get ready for tryouts, and now the big day had arrived. The boys hoping for a spot on the track squad gathered around the new track to stretch and run warm-up laps. The Fellowship of Christian Athletes gathered near the starting line to say a prayer that God would be glorified in their running. They prayed for the opportunity to show Christ's love in their involvement and for the toughness and joy they needed in competition. The tryout for runners would be a three-kilometer run. Runners had to finish under the coach's specified time in order to make the team. Ernest was ready. Not only had he trained, he had some special secret weapons.

The time had come. Ernest lined up. He knew he should be there. After all, whom was he going to believe? "But those who hope in the LORD will renew their strength. They will soar on wings like eagles; they will run and not grow weary, they will walk and not be faint."

The starting gun sounded, and they were off!